BBC

VOLUME 8

EZRA NEHEMIAH and ESTHER

Brady Whitehead, Jr.

ABINGDON PRESS
Nashville

Ezra, Nehemiah, and Esther

Copyright © 1988 by Graded Press

This book is printed on recycled, acid-free paper.

Library of Congress Cataloging-in-Publication Data

Cokesbury basic Bible commentary.
  Basic Bible commentary / by Linda B. Hinton . . . [et.al.].
      p.   cm.
  Originally published: Cokesbury basic Bible commentary. Nashville: Graded Press, © 1988.
  ISBN 0-687-02620-2 (pbk. : v. 1 : alk. paper)
  1. Bible—Commentaries. I. Hinton, Linda B. II. Title.
  [BS491.2.C65   1994]
  220.7—dc20   94-10965
                                                                                    CIP

ISBN 0-687-02627-X (v. 8, Ezra–Esther)
ISBN 0-687-02620-2 (v. 1, Genesis)
ISBN 0-687-02621-0 (v. 2, Exodus–Leviticus)
ISBN 0-687-02622-9 (v. 3, Numbers–Deuteronomy)
ISBN 0-687-02623-7 (v. 4, Joshua–Ruth)
ISBN 0-687-02624-5 (v. 5, 1–2 Samuel)
ISBN 0-687-02625-3 (v. 6, 1–2 Kings)
ISBN 0-687-02626-1 (v. 7, 2 Chronicles)
ISBN 0-687-02628-8 (v. 9, Job)
ISBN 0-687-02629-6 (v. 10, Psalms)
ISBN 0-687-02630-X (v. 11, Proverbs–Song of Solomon)
ISBN 0-687-02631-8 (v. 12, Isaiah)
ISBN 0-687-02632-6 (v. 13, Jeremiah–Lamentation)
ISBN 0-687-02633-4 (v. 14, Ezekiel–Daniel)
ISBN 0-687-02634-2 (v. 15, Hosea–Jonah)
ISBN 0-687-02635-0 (v. 16, Micah–Malachi)
ISBN 0-687-02636-9 (v. 17, Matthew)
ISBN 0-687-02637-7 (v. 18, Mark)
ISBN 0-687-02638-5 (v. 19, Luke)
ISBN 0-687-02639-3 (v. 20, John)
ISBN 0-687-02640-7 (v. 21, Acts)
ISBN 0-687-02642-3 (v. 22, Romans)
ISBN 0-687-02643-1 (v. 23, 1–2 Corinthians)
ISBN 0-687-02644-X (v. 24, Galatians–Ephesians)
ISBN 0-687-02645-8 (v. 25, Philippians–2 Thessalonians)
ISBN 0-687-02646-6 (v. 26, 1 Timothy–Philemon)
ISBN 0-687-02647-4 (v. 27, Hebrews)
ISBN 0-687-02648-2 (v. 28, James–Jude)
ISBN 0-687-02649-0 (v. 29, Revelation)
ISBN 0-687-02650-4 (complete set of 29 vols.)

99 00 01 02 03—10 9 8 7 6 5 4 3 2

MANUFACTURED IN THE UNITED STATES OF AMERICA

Contents

Outline of Ezra, Nehemiah, and Esther

The Book of Ezra

I. The Return From Exile (1:1–2:70)
   A. The proclamation of Cyrus (1:1-4)
   B. Gifts for the Temple (1:5-11)
   C. The people who returned (2:1-70)
II. Rebuilding Begun and Interrupted (3:1–4:24)
   A. The rebuilding begun (3:1-13)
   B. Opposition stops the rebuilding (4:1-24)
      1. Opposition from Cyrus to Darius (4:1-5)
      2. Later opposition (4:6-24)
III. Rebuilding Resumed and Completed (5:1–6:22)
   A. Work on the Temple Is Resumed (5:1-17)
      1. The work resumed (5:1-2)
      2. An investigation of the work (5:3-5)
      3. Tattenai's letter to Darius (5:6-17)
   B. The Temple is completed (6:1-22)
      1. The decree of Cyrus is found (6:1-5)
      2. Darius's reply to Tattenai (6:6-12)
      3. The Temple is dedicated (6:13-18)
      4. The Passover is celebrated (6:19-22)
IV. Ezra's Return (7:1–8:36)
   A. Ezra's genealogy and qualifications (7:1-6)
   B. Ezra's arrival in Jerusalem (7:7-10)
   C. The letter from Artaxerxes (7:11-28)
   D. Those returning with Ezra (8:1-20)
   E. Final preparations for the trip (8:21-30)
   F. Ezra's arrival in Jerusalem (8:31-36)
V. Ezra's Reforms (9:1–10:44)
   A. The problem stated (9:1-2)
   B. Ezra sits appalled (9:3-5)
   C. Ezra's prayer (9:6-15)

EZRA, NEHEMIAH, AND ESTHER

VII. Nehemiah's Reforms (13:1-31)
    A. Separation from foreigners (13:1-3)
    B. The cleansing of the Temple (13:4-9)
    C. Restoration of the Levites (13:10-14)
    D. Enforcement of the sabbath laws (13:15-22)
    E. Purification from foreign influence (13:23-29)
    F. Nehemiah's accomplishments (13:30-31)

The Book of Esther

I. Esther Becomes Queen (1:1–2:23)
    A. King Ahasuerus gives three banquets (1:1-9)
    B. Queen Vashti is deposed (1:10-22)
    C. Esther selected as the new queen (2:1-18)
    D. Mordecai notifies the king of danger (2:19-23)
II. Haman's Plot and Esther's Determination (3:1–4:17)
    A. Haman's plot against the Jews (3:1-15)
        1. Haman's promotion, Mordecai's defiance (3:1-4)
        2. Haman's retaliation (3:5-15)
    B. Esther sees the king (4:1-17)
III. Haman's Humiliation (5:1–6:14)
    A. Esther's first banquet (5:1-8)
    B. Haman's plot against Mordecai (5:9-14)
    C. Mordecai is honored (6:1-14)
        1. The king decides to honor Mordecai (6:1-6a)
        2. Haman describes the perfect honor (6:6b-9)
        3. Haman is humiliated (6:10-14)
IV. Haman Loses His Life (7:1-10)
    A. Haman is accused (7:1-6)
    B. Haman pleads for his life (7:7-8)
    C. A third accusation (7:9-10)
V. The Feast of Purim (8:1–10:3)
    A. A second royal edict (8:1-17)
    B. The slaughter of the enemies (9:1-15)
    C. The celebration of Purim (9:16-32)
    D. The greatness of Mordecai (10:1-3)

Introduction to Ezra

Except for the books of Ezra and Nehemiah, our knowledge of the Israelite people in those formative years immediately following the Babylonian Exile would be virtually nil. We would know nothing of the return from the Exile, almost nothing of the rebuilding of the Temple and those who inspired this work, and nothing of the Samaritan opposition which began here, but lingered and festered for centuries afterward (see John 4:9).

We would have no information about the repopulation of Jerusalem and the reconstruction of the city walls. We would know nothing of the reforms under Nehemiah and Ezra, which rid the Israelite religion of pagan influences and protected it from foreign divinities. Most importantly, we would have no knowledge of Ezra's reading of the law to the people and of their acceptance of it as God's authoritative word, which, if our understanding of that event is correct, marks the true beginning both of Judaism as a religion and the formation of the Jewish Bible. The books of Ezra and Nehemiah, then, command a place of special honor among the books of the Bible.

The Origin of the Book

When first written, and for centuries afterward, Ezra and Nehemiah stood as one book, called Ezra. Not until the time of Origen (third century) do we have evidence that the book had been divided into two parts. The Book of Ezra/Nehemiah is related to the books of 1 and 2

Chronicles, which originally stood as one book, called The Chronicles. The relationship, in fact, is so close that many scholars believe all four of these books were originally one book. The language and writing style are the same in all four books, and so are the dominant interest and the theological point of view. Additionally, the book of Ezra begins exactly where 2 Chronicles leaves off, even repeating the decree which ends that book (see 2 Chronicles 36:22-23 and Ezra 1:1-4).

The Author

An ancient Jewish tradition says that Ezra himself was responsible for writing these four books, and modern scholarship finds much to commend that ancient belief. But there are also difficulties with this view. Most scholars call the author *The Chronicler*, preferring the awkwardness of that name to the uncertainty of the identification with Ezra.

Who Came First—Ezra or Nehemiah?

The careful reader of the books of Ezra and Nehemiah may well become confused. Events that at first glance seem to be connected with the story just read appear, upon closer reflection, to be related instead to a story told elsewhere in the book. Episodes are related out of chronological sequence, and similar types of action are told one after the other although the events themselves may have happened years, or even decades, apart.

One of the most baffling problems of chronology is whether Ezra or Nehemiah came to Jerusalem first. The present order of the material leaves the impression that Ezra did. Ezra left Babylonia in the seventh year of the reign of King Artaxerxes (Ezra 7:1, 6-7); thirteen years later Nehemiah returned to Jerusalem (Nehemiah 1:1; 2:1); the two men were there together for an undetermined length of time (Nehemiah 8:1, 9).

However, there are many indications that Nehemiah returned to Jerusalem before Ezra did. For example:

(1) When Nehemiah returned to Jerusalem, he found the city to be sparsely settled (Nehemiah 7:4), and he had to take measures to repopulate it (Nehemiah 11:1-2). By the time Ezra arrived, however, Jerusalem seems to have had a large number of people living in it (Ezra 10:1).

(2) Nehemiah had to rebuild the city wall after he arrived (Nehemiah 2:11-12, 16-17). In Ezra's day, the wall seems to have been already standing (Ezra 9:9).

(3) Nehemiah had to appoint people to act as Temple treasurers (Nehemiah 13:13), whereas a group of priests was already acting in that capacity when Ezra first arrived (Ezra 8:33).

(4) Eliashib was the high priest at the time of Nehemiah (Nehemiah 3:1, 20), whereas Jehohanan, the son of Eliashib (or perhaps the grandson; see Nehemiah 12:10-11 and 13:28) seems to have been the high priest at the time of Ezra (Ezra 10:6).

(5) None of the persons who returned to Jerusalem with Ezra (Ezra 8:1-20), nor any of their children, are reported to have assisted Nehemiah in the rebuilding of the wall (Nehemiah 3:1-32). Nehemiah 2:17-18 gives the impression that all the people were eager to help. It seems especially incredible that those who returned with Ezra would not have helped in that project had they been there at the time the work was being done.

(6) Ezra left Babylon with the law book in his hand (Ezra 7:6, 14, 25). He was eager to teach the law to the people (Ezra 7:10), and he had full authority to command obedience to it (Ezra 7:25-26). Why, then, would he wait thirteen years, until Nehemiah arrived (Nehemiah 8:9), to do so? The more natural explanation is that Nehemiah had preceded Ezra to Jerusalem.

There are other reasons, too, for believing Nehemiah returned to Jerusalem before Ezra did, including supporting evidence from an archaeological find (discussed in the Introduction to Nehemiah). None of these arguments is conclusive, not even all of them together, but they certainly point in that direction.

But if Nehemiah actually preceded Ezra, why are we told that Ezra returned the seventh year of Artaxerxes, and Nehemiah the twentieth? The answer seems to lie in the fact that three Persian monarchs ruled under the name Artaxerxes. If we assume Nehemiah returned the twentieth year of Artaxerxes I (465–424 B.C.), and Ezra the seventh year of Artaxerxes II (404–358 B.C.), that would place Nehemiah's arrival in 445 and Ezra's in 397.

Historical Background

The Babylonian Empire had only one great leader—its founder and first king, Nebuchadnezzar. At Nebuchadnezzar's death in 562 B.C., there was no strong leader to take his place. Two weak kings later, Nabonidus came to the Babylonian throne. Though he reigned in name some sixteen years (555–539 B.C.), his son, Belshazzar, was the actual ruler most of that time. In 539 Cyrus, the Elamite king whose political shrewdness far outmatched that of either Nabonidus or Belshazzar, wrested the empire from their hands with hardly a drop of blood shed.

Cyrus was a more enlightened ruler than the kings of Babylon had been. Nebuchadnezzar's policy, followed by all his successors, was to take the leaders of the conquered nations into exile in order to minimize the risk of insurrection. Cyrus's philosophy was different. He believed people are easiest to rule when they are happy, and they are happy when they are allowed to live in their own land and worship their own gods. Shortly after his takeover of the empire, therefore, Cyrus issued an edict allowing the exiles within his empire to return to their homelands and rebuild their temples. Among those enjoying this privilege were the exiles from Judah.

Ezra 1–2

Introduction to These Chapters

In these first two chapters of the book of Ezra, the writer has provided several different kinds of information. The book opens with a decree issued by Cyrus, king of Persia. These chapters also contain lists of returnees from the Exile, names of cities in Judah, names of Temple servants, and a list of miscellaneous persons not included on any of the other lists.

Here is an outline of these chapters.

I. The Proclamation of Cyrus (1:1-4)
II. Gifts for the Temple (1:5-11)
III. A Census of Those Returning (2:1-20)
IV. Names of Cities in Judah (2:21-35)
V. Names of Temple Servants (2:36-58)
VI. Names of Others Are Listed (2:59-63)
VII. Conclusion (2:64-70)

The Proclamation of Cyrus (1:1-4)

The book of Ezra begins exactly where the book of 2 Chronicles left off—with the decree of Cyrus, allowing the Jews to return to their homeland and rebuild their Temple. This decree is found in 2 Chronicles 36:23, here in Ezra 1:2-4, and in the apocryphal book I Esdras 2:3-7. It also appears in slightly different form in Ezra 6:3-5.

The first word of the Hebrew text is left untranslated in the NRSV and NIV. This word means *at this time.*

The first year of Cyrus refers to his first year as ruler

over the Jews, 539 B.C. It is not clear what word of . . .
Jeremiah is being referred to. Jeremiah had predicted the
defeat of Babylon (Jeremiah 25:11-12; 51:11), had
indicated that the Judahites would return to their
homeland (Jeremiah 29:10), and had said that Jerusalem
would be rebuilt (Jeremiah 31:38). Any or all of these
promises might have been in the author's mind.

The LORD *stirred up the spirit* (NRSV) or *moved the heart*
(NIV) *of Cyrus.* The biblical writers were convinced that
their God, the one true God, controlled the destiny of all
the world. Even kings of foreign nations obeyed God's
voice.

The king made *a proclamation* (more literally, he made
a voice pass) throughout all his kingdom. That is, the
king *sent heralds* (NRSV) to proclaim the decree. In
addition, however, he also put it in writing.

The biblical version of Cyrus's decree sounds as if it
were meant for Judahites only. We know from Cyrus's
writings, however, (on what is known as the *Cyrus
Cylinder*) that he allowed the captives of other nations,
too, to return to their homes and rebuild their temples.
There is no hint from Cyrus that the people of Judah
were treated any differently from others in his empire.

The LORD (verse 2) translates *Yahweh*, the name of the
Israelite God. Why would Cyrus, an Elamite, give credit
to the Israelite God for his victories? Some have seen this
as evidence that this is a Jewish paraphrase of the edict.
On the Cyrus Cylinder, however, credit is given to the
god Marduk. And on a text from Ur, it is the moon-god,
Sin, who is credited with the victories. Perhaps Cyrus's
policy was to give credit to the god of the people he was
addressing.

All *survivors* (verse 4) refer to those Judahites who had
survived the ravages of Nebuchadnezzar (see
2 Kings 25:8-12; 2 Chronicles 36:17-20), had weathered
the captivity in Babylon, and were now being allowed to
return home. That much is clear. But who are meant by

EZRA, NEHEMIAH, AND ESTHER

the *people* of any *place*? If each survivor is literally every Judahite in exile, then those called upon to assist *with silver and gold* would either be the Babylonians and other non-Jews living in Babylonia, or the Judahites who were never taken into exile. It does not seem reasonable, however, to expect the Babylonians to finance the Jews' trip back home. Nor does it seem possible that those left in Jerusalem could do so, since only *the poorest people of the land* were left behind (2 Kings 25:11-12).

The pieces fall into place if we consider each survivor as those Judahites who are returning, and *the people of any place* as those who chose to remain in Babylon. Jeremiah had advised the exiles to settle down in Babylon, and lead normal lives there (see Jeremiah 29:1, 4-7). Many had done so, with the result that some of them had prospered financially. For these people, the long trek back to Jerusalem, and the prospects of having to start over financially, had little appeal. They chose to remain in Babylon. It was these wealthier Judahites who were asked to finance the trip of those who were returning. There surely were many who were eager to do so.

There is yet another possibility, however. The biblical writers were struck with the similarity between God's leading the people out of slavery in Egypt, and God's leading the people back home from exile. Etched in the memory of the Israelites was the fact that their ancestors had *plundered the Egyptians* when they left Egypt (Exodus 3:21-22; 12:36). What we have in Ezra 1:4, therefore, may be an attempt to further the parallels between these two saving events. Before leaving Babylon, the Judahites despoiled the Babylonians.

Gifts for the Temple (1:5-11)

The heads of the families houses were the oldest living males of the families. Included in the *family's' houses* were not only the descendants of the families, but also the descendants of their brothers and male cousins, plus any unmarried female descendants.

Judah and Benjamin were the two tribes that formed the nation of Judah, and were therefore the two tribes from which the exiles came.

The origin of the *priests and the Levites* is much disputed. The traditional view is that the priests were descendants of Aaron, the brother of Moses (see Exodus 28:1, 43; Numbers 3:10), and the Levites were the descendants of the remainder of the tribe of Levi, set aside to assist the priests in their duties (Numbers 3:5-9; 18:1-6).

Aided (NRSV) or *Assisted them* (NIV) literally *strengthened their hands* (as in the King James Version). The term is a common one, and means *gave encouragement to* or *strengthened their resolve to* (see, for example, Nehemiah 6:9).

Nebuchadnezzar had plundered the costly Temple vessels (verse 7) when he overran Jerusalem (2 Kings 24:12-13; 25:13-15). *Cyrus* now returns them. Yet a question arises, for Nebuchadnezzar not only took the vessels; he cut them *in pieces* (NRSV) or *took away* (NIV) (2 Kings 24:13), and carted them off, not as vessels, but *as gold* and *as silver* (1 Kings 25:15; see also Jeremiah 52:17-19). How, then, could Cyrus return the vessels? The Chronicler does not address this issue. For him it was important to say the vessels were returned, for he was demonstrating the continuity between the old Temple and the new. Not only would the new Temple be built on the same foundation as the old, but also the same vessels would be used in its services.

Mithredath (verse 8) is a common Persian name, meaning *gift of Mithra*, one of the Persian gods. He undoubtedly was a trusted Persian official.

But who was *Sheshbazzar*? Many suggestions have been made, each with some merit, but none totally convincing. The best solution is to take the words *the prince of Judah* literally. Sheshbazzar was the son of the exiled king, Jehoiachin. We know that Jehoiachin had a son called Shenazzar (see 1 Chronicles 3:16-18). It is not beyond our imagination to suppose that Shenazzar is a nickname for Sheshbazzar, just as Jehoiachin is called by a nickname, *Jeconiah* (see 1 Chronicles 3:16). And even that name is shortened to *Coniah* in Jeremiah 22:24, 28; 37:1.

The vessels mentioned in verse 7 are enumerated in verses 9-11. Two problems emerge. First, there are words in this list which are of uncertain meanings. The words translated as *basins* and *gold bowls* (NRSV) or *silver pans* (NIV) (verse 9) appear only here in the Bible, and are probably Hebrew spellings for Persian or Babylonian words. The word translated as *bowls* appears in the Bible only in the writings of the Chronicler—here, in 8:27, and in 1 Chronicles 28:17.

The second problem is that the total given in the Hebrew text (verse 11) does not match the sum of the vessels listed in verses 9-10. The Revised Standard Version therefore abandons the Hebrew text in these verses, and lists instead the numbers given in 1 Esdras 2:13-14. The numbers in 1 Esdras are consistent, but that is no guarantee that they are correct. The author of 1 Esdras was probably dependent on the book of Ezra for his information, and he may simply have altered the numbers to make the total correct.

A Census of Those Returning (2:1-20)

Chapter 2 begins, *Now these were the people . . . who came up from* captivity. Having just read of a group of returnees in Chapter 1, we naturally expect this to be a list of those persons. However, what we have is a list of those who *came with Zerubbabel* (verse 2). Zerubbabel was the grandson of King Jehoiachin, and the nephew of Shenazzar (see 1 Chronicles 3:16-19).

The sequence of events seems to be this. Sheshbazzar (or Shenazzar, see the comments on 1:8) returned with the first group in 538 B.C. (1:8, 11), and was their governor

(5:14). Under his leadership, work on the Temple began, and the foundation of the Temple was laid (5:16). Soon, however, enthusiasm for the project waned, and work on the Temple stopped, as the people became more concerned to construct nice homes for themselves (Haggai 1:3, 9). In 520 B.C., another group returned from exile, this time under the leadership of Zerubbabel (Ezra 2:2; 3:2), who was their governor (Haggai 1:1, 14; 2:2, 21). Work on the Temple was resumed, and the foundation was laid once again (Ezra 3:8-10; 5:1-2; Zechariah 4:9; Haggai 1:14). Thus, both Sheshbazzar and Zerubbabel led groups back to Jerusalem, both served as governors, both laid the foundation of the Temple, but they did so eighteen years apart.

One of the Chronicler's main concerns was to show that life after the Exile picked up right where it had stopped forty-eight years earlier. Thus, the exiles returned . . . each to his own town (verse 1). We are not to assume, however, that every pre-exilic town was repopulated, or that no new towns were established.

Verse 3 reads the descendants of. More was included, however, than the descendants of just one man. (See the discussion of the heads of the families in 1:5.) Later in the list, some are referred to as the men of (NIV-implied in NRSV) . . . . This phrase designates place names rather than family names. Perhaps the Chronicler has combined two lists. Another possibility is that those who lived in Jerusalem were listed by families, and those who lived outside Jerusalem were listed by towns.

The name Parosh means flea, and is found with that meaning in 1 Samuel 24:14. It is used in a metaphorical sense in 1 Samuel 26:20.

Azgad (verse 12) is an Edomite name meaning Gad is strong. Gad was a god of fortune, and is one of the gods referred to in Isaiah 65:11.

Names of Cities in Judah (2:21-35)

The place names begin here. Only two of the towns listed lay within the bounds of Judah (Bethlehem, verse

21, and *Netophah*, verse 22). All the others were Benjaminite towns. Perhaps the Edomites had taken the depopulated cities of Judah as their own. Certainly the Edomites were glad to see the cities of Judah crushed (see Psalm 137:7, for example).

Bethlehem (verse 21) had been the home of David, and therefore was an honored town. Micah 5:2 was commonly interpreted to mean that the messiah would be born in Bethlehem, and it was this information that *the chief priests and scribes* (NRSV) or *teachers of the law* (NIV) gave Herod in Matthew 2:1-6.

Anathoth (verse 23) was the birthplace of Jeremiah (see Jeremiah 1:1).

Jeremiah pictures *Ramah* (verse 26) as a place of grief, where Rachel weeps for her children (Jeremiah 31:15). Rachel, as the wife of Jacob and the mother of Benjamin (Genesis 35:16-20), was the mother of all the Benjaminites. She is bewailing their captivity and exile at the hands of the Babylonians. The New Testament writer refers to the Jeremiah passage to express the grief of the mothers whose sons Herod had slaughtered (Matthew 2:16-18).

Bethel (verse 28) had played a prominent role in the history of Israel. It was there that Jacob's name was changed to Israel (Genesis 35:1, 10), and there that Amos had his run-in with the priest Amaziah (Amos 7:10-17).

Jericho (verse 34) is famous for the battle Joshua fought there. It was also at Jericho that Zacchaeus climbed a sycamore tree in order to get a better look at Jesus (see Luke 19:1-10).

Names of Temple Servants (2:36-58)

The Chronicler now lists all those who served in the Temple—*priests, Levites, singers, gatekeepers, temple servants,* and *Solomon's servants,* in that order. The number of priests seems unusually high—4,289—approximately one out of ten of those who returned (see verse 64). The number of Levites, on the other hand, is surprisingly low—only seventy-four. What happened to the 38,000 Levites active during the time of David (1 Chronicles 23:3)? A combination of factors seems to have been at work to reduce their number. Central among these was the fact that their whole reason for being was lost during the Exile. Their function was to assist in the Temple, and where there was no Temple, there was no job. Many Levites, therefore, undoubtedly sought secular employment. It is quite possible that some of the laypersons who returned to Jerusalem were former Levites or their descendants. The priesthood would not have suffered the same decline because there were duties other than Temple duties which the priests performed.

Pashhur (verse 38) was the priest who had Jeremiah put in the stocks (Jeremiah 20:1-6).

The singers and the gatekeepers (verses 41-42) were also Levites. *Asaph* was one of the men David put in charge of the music for the Temple (1 Chronicles 6:31-32, 39). Psalms 50 and 73–83 are attributed to him. The gatekeepers were charged with the responsibility of guarding the Temple gates, though other tasks could be assigned to them as well (1 Chronicles 9:23-32). Though not a desirable or prestigious job (as Psalm 84:10 affirms), it was nevertheless an important one because of all the precious altarware in the Temple.

The *temple servants* apparently were given the least desirable tasks in the Temple, though they may have been a notch above *Solomon's servants* (verse 55). Many of the names are foreign, indicating, perhaps, that the Temple servants were prisoners of war. Many of the rest of the names are nicknames such as one might give to a faithful slave.

Apparently, Solomon's servants were the descendants of those whom Solomon took as slaves to build the Temple, his own palace, and other buildings (1 Kings 9:15, 20-21; 2 Chronicles 8:7-8.

Names of Others Are Listed (2:59-63)

In these verses are listed those who . . . could not prove . . . they belonged to Israel. Apparently, their genealogical records were lost in the confusion of the Exile. These records were important, not only because they identified the racially (religiously) pure, but also because they insured that the restored community would be a direct continuation of the old.

The five Babylonian towns mentioned in verse 59 are not as yet identified. The prefix *Tel* means *mound*, and generally is applied to an artificial mound created by the ruins of a city formerly on that spot. *Tel-melah* is *mound of salt*. Conquerors sometimes poured salt on the defeated city to kill the vegetation (see, for example, Judges 9:45). Tel-melah may have been the ruins of such a town. *Tel-harsha* is *mound of silence*, perhaps referring to its refusal to give up its secrets of past life there.

Barzillai is the only man in the Bible of whom it is said he *was called by* his wife's family name. The name means *iron-hearted* or *iron-willed*.

We are not told what happened to the laypersons who could not prove their fathers' houses, but the priests *were excluded from the priesthood as unclean.* Unclean here means unsuited for the task because of possible contamination from foreign deities.

A priest (verse 63) perhaps should read *a high priest,* for there were 4,289 priests available (see verses 36-39). The parallel passage in 1 Esdras 5:40 indicates that a high priest is meant.

The Urim and Thummim were used to determine God's will. They probably were the same as or similar to the ephod (see 1 Samuel 23:9-12; 30:7-8) and the lot (1 Samuel 14:36-42).

Conclusion (2:64-70)

The head count of the whole assembly is given as 42,360. The numbers given in the list, however, total only 29,818. The total of the list in Nehemiah 7 is 31,089, and the total in the corresponding list in 1 Esdras is 31,600. In all three cases, however, the total is said to be 42,360 (Nehemiah 7:66; 1 Esdras 5:41).

Verses 68-69 are an abbreviated and somewhat altered version of the equivalent statement in Nehemiah 7:70-72. The action is once again patterned after the account of the Exodus (see Exodus 25:2-9; 35:21-29).

Darics (Drachmas) (NIV) or (NRSV) were Persian coins, and are the first coins mentioned in the Bible. The *mina* was not a coin, but a unit of weight. Since there was a light mina and a heavy mina, and also since the standard weights changed from time to time, it is impossible to say what sum of money is represented by 5,000 minas of silver.

The priests' garments were made of good quality linen, and embroidered (see Exodus 28:39; 39:27-31). *One hundred* such garments represent considerable work and expense.

§ § § § § § §

The Message of Ezra 1–2

§ God takes the initiative to redeem those God has punished. The people could not save themselves. Cyrus was stirred into action by God's initiative.

§ God uses people when they do not worship the Lord as their God. Cyrus was an Elamite, not an Israelite, and he worshiped the Persian god. Yet, when God *stirred up his spirit*, Cyrus obeyed.

§ God can turn despair into excitement, and hopelessness into exhilaration. We cannot miss the thrill and anticipation that pervade these chapters. At long last, the people's dream will come true. God has acted again! The second Exodus is here.

§ § § § § § §

EZRA, NEHEMIAH, AND ESTHER

Ezra 3–4

Introduction to These Chapters

Chapters 3 and 4 tell of the reinstituting of the religious ceremonies at Jerusalem and about the first attempts at rebuilding the Temple. Here is an outline of Ezra 3–4.

   I. The Rebuilding Begun (3:1-13)
      A. Altar rebuilt and offerings reinstituted (3:1-6)
      B. Laying the Temple foundation (3:7-13)
   II. Opposition Stops the Rebuilding (4:1-24)
      A. Opposition from Cyrus to Darius (4:1-5)
      B. Later opposition (4:6-24)

Altar Rebuilt and Offerings Reinstituted (3:1-6)

The Chronicler's purpose here is to show that the returned community wasted no time in building an altar to God and in presenting offerings there. Yet, those who gathered in Jerusalem were the ones who returned with Zerubbabel, not the first group who returned with Sheshbazzar. Because of this, and for other reasons, some have thought Sheshbazzar and Zerubbabel were the same person. Or perhaps the Chronicler, writing some 140 years after the fact, thought they were the same man, and treated them as such.

The simplest explanation, however, is that the Chronicler's sources of information were limited. He knew of a group that returned with Sheshbazzar, and he recorded that fact. Having no other information about that particular group, he recorded the activities of a group he did have information about, the one that returned with Zerubbabel.

The seventh month, called Tishri (verse 1), corresponds to our September/October. From the earliest times this month was a month of religious significance for the Hebrew people (see Numbers 29:1,7,12).

Jeshua (verse 2) is called Joshua in the books of Haggai and Zechariah.

Zerubbabel is called *the son of Shealtiel* here, and is usually so designated (Ezra 3:8; 5:2; Nehemiah 12:1; Haggai 1:1). In First Chronicles, however, Zerubbabel is listed as the son of Pedaiah, one of the brothers of Shealtiel (1 Chronicles 3:17-19). It is possible that Zerubbabel was the natural son of Pedaiah, but the legal son of Shealtiel because of a levirate marriage (see Deuteronomy 25:5-10).

Nebuchadnezzar had destroyed the altar when he demolished the Temple (2 Kings 25:8-9; 2 Chronicles 36:17-19). According to Jeremiah 41:5, however, the Temple was used even during the Exile. It is likely, therefore, that the altar had been rebuilt. Even so, the returnees from exile would have felt the need to rebuild the altar to ensure its purity. Moreover, it was their desire to rebuild the altar according to *the law of Moses;* a makeshift altar probably would not have been built according to Mosaic instructions.

Notice again the continuity of the new with the old. The altar is set *in its foundation;* that is, in the same place the old altar stood.

It sounds strange that they were afraid of the people surrounding them. These people came in friendship (chapter 4), and offered to help build the Temple. Perhaps it was because they were tearing down the altar these people used.

The feast of tabernacles (NIV) or *Festival of Booths* (NRSV) (verse 4) was also known as the feast of

Tabernacles or Ingathering. It was an autumn festival, originally borrowed from the Canaanites, celebrating the ingathering of the crops. Booths—temporary shelters made of branches and boughs of leafy trees—were constructed in the fields for those gathering the crops. The Hebrews saw in these structures a symbol of the Exodus from Egypt, since the children of Israel lived in booths in the wilderness.

The feast of Booths, therefore, was turned into a celebration of the Exodus, and became one of the three great annual festivals of the Israelite people (see Leviticus 23:42-43). The other two were the Passover and the feast of Weeks.

The words *as it is written, according to the ordinance, as each day required,* and all the appointed feasts or festivals refer to the Mosaic law. The *freewill offering* is in addition to the required offerings, and is an expression of gratitude to God for one's safekeeping or good fortune (see Deuteronomy 16:10). Missing here, but included in a parallel passage in First Esdras (5:52) are the sabbath offerings (see Numbers 28:9-10).

Laying the Temple Foundation (3:7-13)

Several features of this story are reminiscent of the building of the first Temple. The *masons* and the *carpenters*, for example, are Sidonians and Tyrians, as before. The *cedar trees* (NRSV) or *logs* (NIV) are from Lebanon; the workers are paid in kind rather than in cash. The trees are shipped to Joppa. The construction of the Temple begins in the *second month*. Some of these procedures were customary, and it is not surprising that they were repeated. But the repetition also reflects the Chronicler's concern to show the continuity between the old Temple and the new.

When *the builders laid the foundation of the temple of the Lord* was laid (verse 10), a great celebration took place. The Revised Standard Version carries the correct meaning when it speaks of the priests coming forward *in their vestments*. What the Hebrew says, however, is that the priests stood (or came forward) clothed.

The directions of David for this ceremony are not found in the Old Testament.

It is clear that those who wept with a loud voice (verses 12-13) did so out of disappointment. What is not clear is why they were disappointed. The usual explanation, based on Haggai 2:1-3, is that the new Temple did not match Solomon's Temple in splendor and magnificence. But Haggai's words were uttered before the people resumed work on the Temple. After the foundation had been laid, it was obvious that the new Temple was approximately the same size as the old (compare Ezra 6:3 with 1 Kings 6:2). And, it most likely followed the same boundaries. Why, then, was there disappointment?

One possibility is that this celebration, and therefore this mixture of sadness and joy, came after the completion of the Temple rather than after the laying of the foundation. At that time the Temple would be seen for what it was. Then if it did not measure up to Solomon's Temple, the *older* priests and people *who had seen the first house* (NRSV) or *temple* (NIV) might have wept.

Opposition from Cyrus to Darius (4:1-5)

The purpose of these five verses is to explain why the work on the Temple stopped, and the purpose of verses 6-23 is to show that the harassment continued even after the Temple was completed.

The peoples of the land were not *enemies adversaries* (NIV) or (NRSV) at this time, but came to make a friendly offer to help build the Temple (verse 2). By the time the Chronicler wrote, however, they had become enemies of those who returned from the Exile.

Esarhaddon was the king of Assyria from 681 to 669 B.C. He was the grandson of Sargon, who defeated Israel in

722, and sent the people into exile. Esarhaddon followed his grandfather's practice of moving people around within his empire, and had brought these people to Israel.

Why did Zerubbabel and Jeshua refuse the offer of the peoples of the land (verse 3)? There is nothing in the text to suggest that the Samaritans (the people of the land) came with any ill intent. Furthermore, the word *then* in verse 4 would indicate that it was only after this rebuff that the peoples of the land became adversaries.

The excuse used was that *we alone* were commanded by Cyrus to build the Temple. The real reason, however, was that though the people of the land worshiped the God of Israel, they also continued to worship the gods of their ancestors. For them to have helped build the Temple, therefore, would have been to have polluted the Temple from the very first (see 2 Kings 17:24-41).

The people of the land retaliated against this rebuff (verses 4-5). Discouraged *the people of* is literally *weakened the hands of*. This is a Hebrew idiom meaning to frighten or intimidate to the point of inactivity (see Nehemiah 6:9; Isaiah 13:7; Jeremiah 6:24). *Officials Counselors* (NIV) must refer to Persian officials, who were bribed to frustrate the building program. Such activities continued *until the reign of King Darius* or as translated by NIV *until a report could go to Darius.* that is, about the next eighteen years.

Later Opposition (4:6-24)

In this section we have a parenthetical statement on the part of the Chronicler. He said in verse 5 that the work of building the Temple was stopped until the reign of Darius. Now he is going to show that the attempts to frustrate the work of the Israelites continued even beyond that.

Ahasuerus (NRSV) is better known by his Greek name, (NIV) *Xerxes.* He was the son of Darius. This is the only time the Chronicler mentions Xerxes, but he is the same Ahasuerus we read about in the Book of Esther.

No hint is given concerning the nature of the accusation against the Judahites. We know of a revolt by Egypt during these years, and the Judahites may have been sympathetic to this revolt.

In the days of Artaxerxes the harassment continued. It is not clear who *Bishlam, Mithredath, and Tabeel* were.

The last two words of verse 7 are *in Aramaic*, indicating that what follows is written in Aramaic. These words are left untranslated in English versions, since the whole book of Ezra is translated into English. In the Hebrew text, however, the book alternates between Hebrew and Aramaic. Ezra 1:1–4:7 is in Hebrew; 4:8–6:18 is in Aramaic; 6:19–7:11 is in Hebrew; 7:12-26 is in Aramaic; 7:27–10:44 is in Hebrew. Most likely some of the Chronicler's sources were written in Aramaic.

The letter written by Rehum and Shimshai seems to be different from the letter mentioned in verse 7, although the book of First Esdras indicates there was just one letter (1 Esdras 2:16). The letter was probably from Rehum, with Shimshai simply recording what Rehum dictated. Some believe, however, that the term *scribe* (NRSV) referred not to a secretary, but to a high *official*.

A letter sent to Artaxerxes would have arrived within a week. According to early historians, the Persians built smooth roads, and they had fresh horses posted at fourteen-mile intervals for the purpose of carrying the king's mail.

The letter is introduced twice, in verse 8 and in verse 9. In verse 9 a much longer list of people is responsible for the letter. Apparently, these were Persian officials assigned to that satrapy.

Osnappar (NRSV) (verse 10) is probably another name for (or a corruption of the name of) *Ashurbanipal* (NIV), since he was the Assyrian king who defeated and deported the Elamites.

The province Beyond the River (NRSV: translated in the NIV as *The Men of Trans-Euphrates*) refers to that large province west of the Euphrates River, of which Palestine (Judah and Samaria) was a part.

Jerusalem had been rebellious in the past (verse 12) by such actions as Hezekiah's refusal to serve Assyria (2 Kings 18:7) and Zedekiah's rebellion against Babylon (2 Kings 24:20).

The terms *taxes, tribute, and duty* (NIV) or *tribute, custom, and toll* (NRSV)are used here, in 4:20, and in 7:24. They probably refer to three distinct and well-known taxes. The *tribute* would be the money paid by conquered nations; the *custom* (NRSV) was perhaps the *taxes* (NIV) assessed on individuals in the empire; the *toll* (NRSV) or *DUTY* (NIV) may have been the service required of conquered peoples to maintain the excellent road system.

The words *we share the salt of the palace* (NRSV) (verse 14) may refer to a salt covenant made between conquering and conquered nations (see Leviticus 2:13; Numbers 18:19; 2 Chronicles 13:5). More likely, it is an expression indicating complete reliance on, and absolute *obligation* to the palace as translated by the NIV.

The king's dishonor is literally *the king's nakedness*. The term is used metaphorically, and the Revised Standard Version has captured the true meaning.

The words in verse 16 are an obvious exaggeration, and are intended to rouse the king into action.

There was never a time when Israel ruled over the whole *province Beyond the River* (NRSV) or the whole *Trans-Euphrates* (verse 20). It is possible that Assyrian or Babylonian records had so indicated, in order to magnify their own defeat of Israel. Another possibility is that the mighty kings were not Israelites, but Assyrian and Babylonian kings who ruled over Israel.

Some commentators believe that the words until I so order (verse 21) were added later, since they do not appear in the parallel passage in First Esdras (2:28). Possibly, the king was leaving himself a loophole in case he changed his mind later (see Daniel 6; Esther 1:19).

By force (verse 23) probably refers to military enforcement.

In verse 24 the author indicates that he has completed the parenthetical statement begun in verse 6 by repeating the thought of the words just before the parentheses began. Compare verse 5 with verse 24.

§ § § § § § §

The Message of Ezra 3–4

§ Sometimes we speak of doing the lesser of two evils. What we do seems right and necessary under the circumstances, yet we know even as we do it that it is less than the ideal solution. Because it is the lesser of two evils rather than the right thing to do, it often comes back to haunt us. That is the lesson of Ezra 3–4.

Zerubbabel and Jeshua did what seemed to be absolutely necessary to do at the time. Had they allowed the Samaritans (the people of the land) to join with them in rebuilding the Temple, the pure religion of Israel might have become polluted, even to the point of losing its distinctiveness. And Judaism would have become just another religion, hardly distinguishable from the neighboring pagan religions.

Later, Nehemiah and Ezra would follow this same practice of excluding non-Jews both from their religious community and from their individual families. Once again the policy seemed necessary at the time, but once again it was the lesser of two evils. Hidden within this policy were the seeds of those attitudes of self-righteousness, exclusiveness, and legalism which Jesus condemned in the Pharisees of his day (see Matthew 23). The lesser of two evils became a way of life, and led finally to a diseased religion.

§ If the work that is attempted is divinely inspired, no amount of human opposition can prevent its completion.

§ What may seem *rebellious and wicked* (4:12) to those in authority, may actually be God's will.

§ § § § § § §

Ezra 5–6

Introduction to These Chapters

Chapter 5 picks up the story left at 4:5. In Chapter 6 the Temple is completed, and it closes with a celebration of the Passover and unleavened bread.

Here is an outline of Ezra 5–6.
I. Work on the Temple Is Resumed (5:1-17)
  A. The work resumed (5:1-2)
  B. An investigation of the work (5:3-5)
  C. Tattenai's letter to Darius (5:6-17)
II. The Temple Is Completed (6:1-22)
  A. The decree of Cyrus is found (6:1-5)
  B. Darius's reply to Tattenai (6:6-12)
  C. The Temple is completed and dedicated (6:13-18)
  D. The Passover is celebrated (6:19-22)

The Work Resumed (5:1-2)

Sometimes all that is needed to stir people into action are the words of a powerful speaker and the initiative of a strong leader. Haggai and Zechariah provide the words, and Zerubbabel and Jeshua provide the leadership.

What *prophets of God* are referred to—Haggai and Zechariah, or other prophets? Either interpretation is possible. How were they assisting them—by doing manual labor or by firing the people up with their words? Prophetic words unaccompanied by prophetic action soon lose their power to motivate. We may assume, therefore, that the prophets assisted in the construction.

An Investigation of the Work (5:3-5)

This questioning was not a continuation of the harassment described in Chapter 4. At issue there were two groups each claiming to be the rightful heir of the land and the religion. Bitterness and obstinacy may have clouded the judgment of both parties. Here, however, there is an official investigation by the governor of the province Beyond the River. Darius was in the second year of his reign (Haggai 1:1), and Tattenai was eager to please. When he found people in his territory at work on the Temple, therefore, he stopped to ask about it.

We know from non-biblical sources that Ushtani was a satrap of the province Beyond the River. We know that Tattenai was later elevated to the rank of satrap. Therefore, here he was one of Ushtani's subordinates.

The name *Shethar-bozenai* is unknown except in Ezra 5–6, though a Shethar is mentioned in Esther 1:14. It is possible that *bozenai* is a title. Or perhaps it is a reference to a Persian god.

The Aramaic word translated *structure* is of uncertain meaning. See also verse 9.

To have *the eye of their God* (verse 5) upon them was to be blessed by God's favor.

In verse 2, Zerubbabel is the leader of the people. Here, only three verses later, the leaders are *the elders of the Jews*. What has happened to Zerubbabel? Perhaps such exalted claims for him as found in Haggai 2:20-23 help to account for his disappearance. If the Persian government heard that Zerubbabel had taken the title of king, it would have removed his crown immediately.

Tattenai's Letter to Darius (5:6-17)

Tattenai and Shethar-bozenai write to Darius. Their letter contains three points. (1) We found the Judahites rebuilding their Temple, and we questioned them about it (verses 7-10). (2) They claimed that when Cyrus became king, he made a decree that the Temple should be rebuilt, but the Temple has not yet been completed (verses 11-16). (3) Please let us know if what they say is true, and what we should do now (verse 17).

The reference by the Persian officials to the Hebrew God as *the great God* (verse 8) seems strange. The parallel passage in 1 Esdras 6:9 speaks of a great house rather than a great God.

The word translated *large* in the New International Version is of uncertain meaning. It was assumed in the past to mean huge because the word seemed to be from the root meaning *to roll*, the idea being that the stones were too heavy to lift. Recent discoveries, however, have shown that this word was used for small stones as well as large. Perhaps, then, the word refers to the shape (round?) or the type of stone.

Nor are we sure what is meant by timber is laid *in the walls*. Perhaps the ceiling beams are meant, or maybe wood paneling. Some scholars believe it refers to a type of construction in which every third row or so of stones is followed by a row of timber as a protection against earthquakes (see 6:4; see also 1 Kings 6:36 and 7:12).

This work . . . prospers in their hands (NRSV) means that they are *making rapid progress.* (NIV)

The reply of the Judahites in verses 11-16 is much more than a simple answer to the question of verse 3. It is a carefully constructed statement designed to elicit a favorable response from the king. The *great king of Israel* (verse 11) was Solomon.

Cyrus reverses what Nebuchadnezzar had done. The *vessels* (NIV) or *articles* (NRSV) removed by Nebuchadnezzar are restored, and the *house of God* destroyed by him is to be rebuilt.

The last sentence in verse 17 seems to assume that Darius could go contrary to the edict of Cyrus if he so decided. And no doubt he could, for who was there to prevent the king from doing what he wanted? Yet there was a strong tradition among the Persians that no king's order could be revoked.

The Decree of Cyrus Is Found (6:1-5)

Made a decree (NRSV) (verse 1) sounds public and formal. Probably *issued an order* (NIV) is all that is meant.

Before being conquered by Cyrus in 550 B.C., *the province of Media* had been an independent state, with its capital at Ecbatana. Persian kings continued to use Ecbatana for their summer capital because its high elevation offered relief from the summer heat. The fact that Cyrus's edict was found here would indicate that it had been written in the summer of 538.

There are several differences between this version of Cyrus's decree and the version given in 1:2-4. The emphasis here is on the rebuilding of the Temple. The exact dimensions of the Temple are given, and the manner in which the walls are to be built is specified.

It is understandable that a Judahite would refer to 538 B.C. as *the first year of* Cyrus the king's reign, for that was Cyrus's first year to rule over the Jews. However, Cyrus had been a king since 550.

The Hebrew text does not contain the word *concerning*; it says simply *the house* (NRSV) or *Temple* (NIV) of God *at Jerusalem.* That sounds like a title, and it is possible that verses 3-5 constitute one section of a much longer document which gives similar instructions about other temples in other cities. If so, each section would then have a similar title.

A *cubit* (the term used in the NIV) originally was the distance from the elbow to the tip of the middle finger. Later it was standardized at eighteen inches. *Sixty cubits*, therefore, was ninety feet. Only two dimensions of the building are given, though surely the third dimension was included in the original text. Since the Temple was rebuilt on the same site, the original dimensions probably corresponded with the dimensions of Solomon's Temple (see 1 Kings 6:2).

For the information in verse 4, see the commentary on 5:8 concerning the one course of timber. *One* is actually *new* in the Aramaic text, but new cannot be correct. No builder would use green lumber in constructing a wall. Since the words *one* and *new* are very similar in the Aramaic language, then the NRSV and the NIV have emended the text to read *one*.

The cost was to *be paid from the royal treasury*, but there is no record that this was ever done. The money would not come directly from Persia, but from the province Beyond the River. The older and more established governments within that satrapy may have been successful in seeing that their needs were satisfied first.

Darius's Reply to Tattenai (6:6-12)

Darius affirms Cyrus's decree, and indicates that *the work on this temple* (NIV) or *house* should continue. Notice again the emphasis on building the Temple on the same site.

In verses 8-10, the reason for Darius's generosity was not only that the Jews could offer appropriate sacrifices. Darius also wanted to ensure that they would pray for the king and his family. The Hebrew God was not his god, but he sought help from every god he could.

The letter of Darius closes with two threats. The first (verse 11), while harsh, was not unknown in the ancient world. Sennacherib had impaled certain people in his attack on Lachish, and Darius would later impale some 3,000 Babylonians.

To make of *his house . . . a dunghill* (NRSV) or *pile of rubble* (NIV) is symbolic, and should not be taken literally. It does not mean the house shall be made into a latrine, as some have suggested. Nor does it mean the place where the house stood shall become a garbage heap. It refers rather to the complete destruction of the house, and its utter worthlessness as a place of abode. The same Hebrew word translated *dunghill* or *pile of rubble* here is translated *ruins* (in NIV) in Daniel 2:5 and 3:29.

Many commentators believe verse 12 was not a part of the original letter. Two threats hardly seem necessary.

Furthermore, *God who has caused* (NIV) or *established* (NRSV) *his name* to dwell there is a typically Jewish expression (see Deuteronomy 12:11; 14:23, for example). And finally, it seems unlikely that a Persian monarch would pronounce a curse on someone who sought to destroy a Jewish temple.

To be done with all diligence is to be done carefully, thoroughly, and swiftly.

The Temple Is Completed and Dedicated (6:13-18)

Darius's decree paves the way for the completion of the Temple. Then follows the dedication service and the instituting of the priestly and levitical orders.

According to verse 14, the Temple was completed by the command of God, by the decrees of Cyrus, Darius, and Artaxerxes, and by the encouragement of the prophets Haggai and Zechariah. God, Persian kings, Jewish prophets, and common laborers all combined to build the Second Temple.

The inclusion of the name *Artaxerxes* is surprising. We know of the decrees of both Cyrus and Darius, but the only information we have on Artaxerxes has been negative—the halting of the work on the walls of the city (4:7-23). The Chronicler, however, wrote at a much later time. He knew of the experiences of Nehemiah and Ezra (Nehemiah 2:1-8; Ezra 7:11-28). Thus, just as he had outlined the Samaritan harassment from the time of Cyrus to the time of Artaxerxes (4:6-23), so now he tells of the royal aid during that same period.

Verses 16-17 state that at the completion of the Temple the people celebrated. The celebration is patterned after the dedication of Solomon's Temple, though it is much less grandiose in scale (see 2 Chronicles 7:5).

There are no provisions (verse 18) in *the book of Moses* (the Pentateuch) for setting *the priests in their divisions* or *the Levites in their groups* (NIV) or courses. This was done, according to 1 Chronicles 23–26, not by Moses, but by David.

This completes the first Aramaic section of Ezra

(4:8–6:18). Beginning at 6:19, the text is again written in Hebrew.

The Passover Is Celebrated (6:19-22)

The dedication of the Temple was held in Adar (see 6:15), the last month of the year (our February/March). The *fourteenth day of the first month* was commanded in Exodus 12:1-11 as the time for this celebration.

Verse 20 presents some difficulties, for if the *priests and Levites* were all clean, it is not clear who killed the Passover lamb for whom, or why the priests could not perform these duties. The confusion is cleared up if the words *the priests and* are omitted. Then the Levites would have been the ones to kill the lamb for the priests.

The Passover lamb was eaten not only by those who had returned from exile, but also by anyone who had become separated from the pollutions of the peoples of the land. The returned community, at least at this point, was not as exclusive as it is sometimes made out to be.

The feast of Unleavened Bread follows immediately after the Passover, and lasts for seven days.

The *king of Assyria* is clearly a reference to Darius. Perhaps he is not called the king of Persia because the Persian Empire is really just a continuation of the old Assyrian Empire. By emphasizing this point, the Chronicler may also be pointing out that the returned exiles were related not just to the southern Judahites, but also to the northern Israelites, exiled by the Assyrians.

The Chronicler already has referred to the people of Israel in verse 21, rather than those from the tribes of Judah and Benjamin. And in verse 17 he has said that the sin offering was for *all Israel*, requiring twelve he-goats, one for each of the twelve tribes. The Chronicler is showing that God's concern is for all Israel. The evil done to northern Israel by the Assyrian king and to Judah by the Babylonian king is now being undone by God through the Persian king. On this high note, the first major section of the Book of Ezra comes to a close.

§ § § § § § §

The Message of Ezra 5–6

§ The Chronicler never dreamed that his words would become a part of the Jewish and Christian Scriptures. He wrote in order to help the people of his own day understand how God words through the currents of history to accomplish the divine will. In so doing, however, he left that same message for untold generations to come.

§ It was not Darius who, on his own, decreed that the Temple be rebuilt, but the Lord, the God of Israel and the God of the whole world, who *turned the heart of the king* (NRSV) or *changed the attitude* (NIV) to be favorable toward the Israelites (6:22). In the same way, God had stirred up the spirit of Cyrus to let the people return to their land (1:1).

§ Haggai and Zechariah did not goad the people to rebuild the Temple because of nationalistic fervor, but because they prophesied at the bidding of and in the name of God.

§ Haggai and Zechariah not only spoke God's words of judgment (as, for example, in Haggai 1:3-6), but they also worked beside the people, helping them to rebuild the Temple.

§ It was not by chance that the work on the Temple prospered, but it was because the hand of God was in it.

§ The Temple was completed not because of the skill of the workers or the determination of the people, but because of the command of God.

§ We often explain the events of the world by referring to human motivations and human deeds. But the Chronicler reminds us of a deeper cause—the God who plants the desires in our hearts and calls us into action.

§ § § § § § §

EZRA, NEHEMIAH, AND ESTHER

Ezra 7–8

Introduction to These Chapters

Chapter 7 begins the second major part of the book of Ezra. Here we are introduced to the man Ezra for the first time. We shall be occupied with the work of Ezra for the remainder of the book, and we shall also find a part of his story in the book of Nehemiah (Nehemiah 8–10).

Later rabbis would look back on Ezra as the greatest man of his age. Although modern scholars find reason to doubt some of the achievements his admirers have attributed to him, certainly Ezra was a towering figure of his day, and of extreme importance in setting the direction of post-exilic Judaism.

Here is an outline of Ezra 7–8.
  I. Ezra's Genealogy and Qualifications (7:1-6)
 II. Ezra's Arrival in Jerusalem (7:7-10)
III. The Letter from Artaxerxes (7:11-28)
 IV. Those Returning with Ezra (8:1-20)
  V. Final Preparations for the Trip (8:21-30)
 VI. Ezra's Arrival in Jerusalem (8:31-36)

Ezra's Genealogy and Qualifications (7:1-6)

The chapter begins now after this, but we have to ask, now after what? If Ezra came to Jerusalem in the seventh year of Artaxerxes II, then we have a gap of some 118 years between chapters 6 and 7. And even if we say Ezra returned during the seventh year of Artaxerxes I, there is still a period of fifty-seven years unaccounted for.

The reason for this hiatus is not hard to discover. The Chronicler's concern is not history, but religion. He has given us the details of the struggle to get the Temple rebuilt. The next task was to mold the life of the community around the laws of God. So the Chronicler turns his attention to Ezra, the one who was primarily responsible for that achievement.

Seraiah was the high priest at the time of the Exile (2 Kings 25:18). For a more complete genealogy of Ezra, see 1 Chronicles 6:3-15.

The Chronicler's sentence begun in verse 1, and interrupted by the genealogy, is resumed in verse 6.

Originally, a *scribe* (NRSV) or *teacher* (NIV) was the secretary of a king and a member of his royal court. It was the scribe's duty to record the king's edicts and the official history of the country during the king's reign. During the Exile, however, the term scribe came to be associated particularly with the study, interpretation, and teaching of the law. It is in this sense that Ezra is called *a scribe* NRSV or *teacher* (NIV).

Ezra's Arrival in Jerusalem (7:7-10)

The trip took 110 days (subtracting the twelve days mentioned in 8:31). Since the route from Babylon to Jerusalem was approximately 900 miles long, the distance covered each day was a little over eight miles, or about ten miles a day if the people did not travel on the sabbath.

Ezra devoted himself (NIV) or . . . *set his heart*, that is, determined with his whole being, *to study* the Scriptures (*the law of the* LORD), to live by them (*to do it*) and to teach God's laws in Israel.

The Letter from Artaxerxes (7:11-28)

The letter of Artaxerxes, which is written in Aramaic, divides rather naturally into three sections. Verses 12-20 give Ezra (and others) permission to return to Jerusalem to determine how scrupulously the people are living by God's law (verse 14). Verses 21-24 are addressed to the treasurers in the province Beyond the River, and indicate that they are to provide Ezra with whatever he needs for his work. Verses 25-26 are once again addressed to Ezra, and give him the authority to appoint magistrates and judges who shall make sure the laws of God and king are obeyed.

The law of the God of heaven is the same as *the law of the* LORD in verse 10, *the law of Moses* in verse 6, *the law of your God* in verse 14, and *the wisdom of your* (NIV) or *God-given wisdom* (NRSV) God in verse 25. It was from this document that Ezra read in Chapter 8 of Nehemiah.

The inquiries which Ezra was to make . . . *about Judah and Jerusalem* were to determine how meticulously the people were obeying *the law of your God*.

How could Artaxerxes have such precise knowledge concerning the needs of the Jewish sacrificial system (verse 17)? One possibility is that Artaxerxes had help from a Babylonian Jew, perhaps Ezra himself, in compiling the list of sacrificial needs.

The phrase *with all diligence* (NRSV) or *be sure to* (NIV) translates an Aramaic word, meaning *precisely* or *exactly*. The thought seems to be that the money is to be used for that purpose, and no other.

Your brother Jews (NIV) or *colleagues* (NRSV) (verse 18) means your fellow priests.

The treasurers in the province Beyond the River (NRSV) or *of the Trans-Euphrates* (NIV) are to provide whatever Ezra needs up to certain limits. *Salt*, however, may be given to Ezra without limit, either because salt was plentiful and inexpensive or because not much salt was required.

A hundred talents of silver was a huge sum. The annual tax for the entire satrapy, according to Herodotus, was only 350 talents of silver. It does not sound plausible that Artaxerxes would require that 28 per cent of that amount be devoted to Jewish worship needs.

Just as earlier Darius desired the prayers of the Jewish priests for himself and his sons (6:10), so here Artaxerxes does not want to offend the God of the Jews lest his wrath be against the realm of the king and his sons (verse 23).

It was not unheard of for a Persian king to exempt priests of a foreign cult from paying taxes. Darius had done the same for the priests of Apollo.

It was stated in verse 6 that the king granted Ezra all that he had asked. The provisions of verses 13-24 give us our best clue as to what these requests were.

It seems strange that *Ezra* was given the authority to *appoint magistrates and judges* (the distinction between these two terms is unknown) to enforce *the laws of your God*. Why would a Persian king be concerned with that? It sounds even more out of the ordinary for Ezra to have the authority to appoint those who were to see that *the law of the king* was upheld. Why wouldn't the king himself appoint such persons?

There are two possible explanations. If Ezra was an official in the Persian Empire, then it would not be unusual for Artaxerxes to entrust these responsibilities to him. The other possibility has to do with politics. Egypt was always a threat to any Mesopotamian monarch. Since the province Beyond the River was adjacent to Egypt, Artaxerxes may have been courting Ezra's favor as a way of securing his loyalty to the empire.

Four punishments are prescribed for offenders. They are listed in descending order of severity—*death . . . banishment . . . confiscation of his goods* (NRSV) or *property* (NIV) . . . *imprisonment*. Since the Aramaic script did not use vowels, it is sometimes difficult to know which word is meant. By using the same consonants, but different vowels, the word translated *banishment* can become a Persian loan word meaning *corporal punishment*. Some scholars see this as a preferable translation.

Beginning at verse 27, the book is once again written in Hebrew. Also beginning here are the *memoirs of Ezra*, one of the Chronicler's sources.

One has only to read verse 27 to realize that we do not have the Ezra memoirs in their entirety. They would not have begun as this verse reads. Probably the information found in 7:1, 6-10, and possibly the information in verses 12-26, was taken from Ezra's memoirs.

Those Returning with Ezra (8:1-20)

In contrast to the list of chapter 2, the priests are listed first here. This is the more usual order.

Hattush is identified in the Ezra memoirs as being *of the sons of David*. Zerubbabel, who was much more prominent than Hattush, was also of the lineage of David, but that fact was never mentioned (see 3:2).

Of the descendants of Shecaniah (verse 3) is obviously an error, for it is an incomplete sentence. Either there should be a name following *Shecaniah*, or, as in the parallel passage in First Esdras, the verse should read, *Hattush the descendant of Shecaniah* (1 Esdras 8:29).

The words *of Zattu* (verse 5) are missing in the Hebrew text of Ezra, but are found in the parallel list in 1 Esdras 8:32. That the words *of Zattu* are correct is confirmed by Ezra 2:8. Similarly, in 8:10, the name *Bani* is missing from the text of Ezra, but is found in 1 Esdras 8:36. That *Bani* is the correct name is confirmed by Ezra 2:10.

Jeshaiah (verse 7) is an alternate spelling of *Isaiah*. The reference, however, is not to the great prophet of that name.

The Greek form of *Zebadiah* (verse 8) is *Zebedee*, the name of the father of two of Jesus' disciples (see Mark 1:19-20 and parallels).

Those who came later (NRSV) (8:13) is a translation of one Hebrew word, a word that literally means *the last ones*. (NIV) Perhaps the meaning is that these are the last names in the list. If so, what about the names in verse 14? Perhaps some of the *Adonikam* family had gone to Jerusalem earlier. However, that is true of most of the other families, so why single out this family? Is the meaning that no more of the Adonikam family now remains in Babylon? Perhaps, but we cannot be sure. Almost certainly, however, the word does not mean *those who came later*.

Neither *Ahava* nor *the river that runs to* (NRSV) or *the Canal that flows to it* (NIV) it can be identified with any certainty.

Three of the eleven men listed in verse 16 were named *Elnathan*, and a fourth is called *Nathan*, a variant of the same name. Further, two of the remaining seven were named *Joiarib*, one going by the shortened form *Jarib*. This has caused some commentators to believe that some errors have crept into the text.

A second problem is that the first nine listed are called *leaders*, while the last two are called *men of learning* (NIV) or *wise* (NRSV). The second problem would be solved, and the first problem helped considerably, if the words *and for Joiarib and Elnathan* were omitted.

The place Casiphia (NRSV-implied in NIV) (verse 17) is unknown except for this one mention of it. It is possible that a Jewish temple was there, since the word *place* is sometimes used in the Old Testament to refer to the Temple in Jerusalem (see Deuteronomy 12:5, 11; 14:23; 1 Kings 8:29; Jeremiah 7:3, 6, 7).

Ministers (NRSV) or *attendants* (NIV) refer to Levites, not priests.

Ezra said it was *by the gracious hand of our God* that Iddo was able to secure *Sherebiah* to go with them. Judging by the prominent role that Sherebiah played after his return to Jerusalem, it would seem that Ezra was right (see Ezra 8:24; Nehemiah 8:7; 9:4, 5; 10:12; 12:8, 24).

Apparently Ezra has a list of *temple servants* (verse 20), but he does not include that list here. Since Ezra was searching only for Levites, either the *temple servants* volunteered to go, or the Levites refused to go without them.

Final Preparations for the Trip (8:21-30)

The *fast* was to seek God's protection. Here *the canal* (NIV) or *river* (NRSV) is named *Ahava*, whereas in verse 15, the town was. *All our possessions* was a considerable sum (see 7:15, 19; 8:25-27).

Although we would like to think Ezra's refusal to ask for a military escort was because of his strong faith, Ezra confesses that it was a way of saving face. *He was ashamed to ask . . . for* an escort because of all the talking he had done. What is strange, however, is that Artaxerxes allowed the caravan to go unprotected, since the priests were taking so much gold and silver from the treasury.

At first glance, verse 24 seems to be talking only about twelve priests. But *Sherebiah* and *Hashabiah* were both Levites (see verses 18-19). *Ten of their* brothers would be ten other Levites. Apparently, then, Ezra *set apart twelve . . . leading priests* and twelve Levites.

The word *holy* (NRSV) *concecrated* (NIV) (verse 28) means *set apart for God*. The priests and Levites are holy, and now the vessels or bowls are holy, for they have been set apart for use in the service of God.

For a description of *the chambers* of Solomon's Temple (verse 29), see 1 Kings 6:5-6. The Second Temple probably followed the same design.

The Second Account of Ezra's Arrival in Jerusalem (8:31-36)

Ezra's memoirs undoubtedly contained the exact date of their arrival in Jerusalem, but the Chronicler does not repeat that here, since he has already given us those dates in 7:8-9.

Meremoth the son of Uriah, the priest (verses 33-34) was the grandson of Hakkoz (see Nehemiah 3:4). The sons of Hakkoz were among those who arrived with Zerubbabel, but could not prove descent (Ezra 2:59, 61). Apparently their genealogy was found, for only a highly respected priest would serve as a Temple treasurer.

The narration changes in verse 35 from first person to third person. These verses are comments from the Chronicler rather than part of the memoirs of Ezra.

Seventy-seven is the only number given that is not divisible by twelve. Since it is said specifically that the *twelve bulls* were *for all Israel*, that is, one for each tribe, it is reasonable to suppose that all the numbers originally were divisible by twelve. For that reason, and also because both 1 Esdras (8:66) and Josephus give the number as seventy-two, many scholars believe seventy-two was the original reading.

§ § § § § § §

The Message of Ezra 7–8

There are many lessons for us in these chapters of Ezra, but two stand out in particular.

§ Ezra had set his heart to study the law of the LORD, and to do it . . . (7:10). How often we fail here! It is not that we don't study the Bible. Many of us enjoy reading the stories of the great heroes of our faith. But how many times do these stories stir us into action? How often does studying the Bible lead our Sunday school class into a special community project? Ezra made it plain that studying God's law is not enough; we must also *do it.* Ezra is not alone in this emphasis. (See Deuteronomy 5:1; 11:32; 26:16). The Gospel writers (Matthew 7:24-27) and the rest of the New Testament writers (James 1:25, for example) are equally insistent that studying the Bible is not enough; discipleship requires action. Put quite simply, Bible study that does not result in action is contrary to what the Bible teaches.

§ It is instructive to compare the names of those returning with Ezra (8:2-14) with the names of those who returned earlier with Zerubbabel (2:2-20). Of the eleven families who traveled with Ezra, eight of them were descendants of those who had gone back with Zerubbabel (the numbers are thirteen and ten, respectively, if Zattu and Bani are counted. See the commentary on 8:5). That is 72.7 per cent (or 76.9 per cent counting Zattu and Bani). What better evidence could there be for the truth of Proverbs 22:6, "Train up a child in the way he should go, and when he is old he will not depart from it"? (See also Deuteronomy 6:4-9, 20-25; 11:18-21.) Faith produces faith, generation after generation.

§ § § § § § §

Ezra 9–10

Introduction to these Chapters

In these chapters Ezra requires all the men of Israel who have married foreign women to *put away* these families. The requirement sounds harsh, intolerant, and narrow-minded. Why would Ezra make this requirement? What was wrong with marrying a non-Israelite?

Ezra's actions arose from a concern for religious purity. Israel had been called to be a holy people, a people set apart from the other nations (Exodus 19:3-8). Ezra knew that when an Israelite married a non-Israelite, the danger of apostasy was very real. Even King Solomon had been led into idolatry by his foreign wives (1 Kings 11:1-11). If it could happen to him, it could happen to anybody. The law, therefore, expressly forbade the marrying of the peoples of the land (Deuteronomy 7:1-4). When Ezra discovered that this law had not been kept, he set into motion practices designed to correct the situation which he found intolerable. Ezra's memoirs may have dealt with other improprieties as well, but this is the only one of Ezra's reforms the Chronicler has preserved for us.

Here is an outline of these chapters.
  I. The Problem Stated (9:1-2)
 II. Ezra Sits Appalled (9:3-5)
III. Ezra's Prayer (9:6-15)
 IV. The Response of the People (10:1-5)

The Problem Stated (9:1-2)

The words *after these things* appear to refer to the events just related in chapter 8. Yet, Ezra arrived in Jerusalem on the first day of the fifth month (7:9), and the assembly was not held until the twentieth day of the ninth month (10:9). That leaves four and a half months unaccounted for. What happened during that time? For reasons that are discussed at Nehemiah 8–10, many believe the events described there belong here. Others, however, point out that the delivering of the king's commissions to the satraps and governors (8:36) would have taken considerable time. Perhaps that accounts for the passing of four and a half months.

Some have expressed surprise that Ezra could have been in Jerusalem four and a half months, and not known that some of *the people of Israel and the priests and the Levites* had foreign wives, especially since his commission from the king was to enforce the law of God on the people (7:26). Any pastor can testify, however, that it is possible to be in a church for a longer period than that before discovering certain facts about his or her new congregation. *The peoples of the lands* (NRSV) or *neighboring people* (NIV) were not different in outward appearance, apparently, but only in inward devotion. That kind of difference takes longer to discern.

The list of nations given is patterned after the lists of Exodus 3:8, Deuteronomy 7:1, and other places. By Ezra's time, however, some of these nations no longer existed. Either he is giving a stylized list, or he is emphasizing the continuity between the taking of the land after the Exodus and the resettlement of the land after the Exile. The fact that new nations are added to the conventional list (*the Ammonites, the Moabites,* and *the Egyptians*) would weight the scales toward the latter possibility.

Nothing is said about Israelite women who had married foreign men, presumably because they would leave the community and live as foreigners. The non-Israelite women who had become the *wives* of Israelite men, on the other hand, would join the community, and be the teachers of the children born into these families. Here we see the seeds of that later doctrine that would define a Jew as one born to a Jewish mother.

Perhaps the most despicable aspect of the whole affair was the fact that in this faithlessness the hand of the officials and leaders have led the way. The *officials* doing the wrong obviously are different from the officials of verse 1, who reported the situation to Ezra.

Ezra Sits Appalled (9:3-5)

The tearing of the *garments and . . . mantle*, (NRSV) or *tunic and cloak* (NIV) and the pulling of *hair from* the *head and beard* are all symbols of distress, mourning, horror, or dismay. Having done all these things, Ezra then sat appalled. It is obvious both here and in what follows that Ezra's reaction is not intended as private and personal. He is making a public display of his anguish in the hope of rallying support for his intended actions.

Those who *trembled at the words of . . . God* were those who lived in strict obedience to God's law. The same expression is used in 10:3 and in Isaiah 66:2, 5.

Until the evening sacrifice may simply be a way of indicating how long Ezra sat appalled (see the comparable statement in 1 Kings 18:29, where nothing more than the passing of time is intended). More likely, however, Ezra chose the time of *the evening sacrifice* for its dramatic effect.

The word translated *fasting* (NRSV) (verse 5) literally means humiliation or *self-abasement* (NIV). The New Revised Standard Version assumes *fasting* is meant because the parallel passage in 1 Esdras 8:73 says *fasting*.

Ezra prays on his *knees* with his hands raised *and spread out . . . to the* L ORD. This was a common posture for prayer and probably was the posture assumed by the Pharisee in Jesus' parable, except that he was standing (see Luke 18:10-14).

Ezra's Prayer (9:6-15)

Ezra's prayer has six parts: (1) Israel has sinned (verses 6-7*a*); (2) God has punished Israel (7*b*); (3) God's grace has shone on Israel (8-9); (4) Israel has sinned again (10-14*a*); (5) God's punishment shall come again (14*b*); and (6) a plea for God's grace again (15).

Notice the plural pronouns in verses 6-7: *our iniquities* (NRSV) or *sins* (NIV) . . . *our guilt.* Ezra identifies with his people; their sin is his sin.

In verse 7, Ezra displays the prophetic understanding of history. The disasters that fell upon Israel and Judah came at God's bidding as punishment for the people's sins.

The words *as it is* now do not fit well with what follows (verse 8). They seem to be a later addition to the text, forming a catchword association with verse 6.

In verses 8-9, God's punishment is followed by *a brief moment* of God's favor or grace. This *moment* has been 141 years, if we are correct in assigning Ezra to the time of Artaxerxes II, or eighty years if Artaxerxes I is meant. In either case, this length of time is but a *moment* when compared to the three centuries of Assyrian/Babylonian domination.

A firm place (NIV) or *stake* (NRSV) is literally a tent peg. That terminology comes from the life of nomads. *A secure hold* is not a bad paraphrase, but perhaps indicates a bit more permanence than the Hebrew allows.

To *brighten* (NRSV) or *give light to* (NIV) one's eyes is to bring joy and hope to that person.

Protection (NIV) is literally a wall. The NRSV takes the meaning to be metaphorical. It is possible, however, that

Ezra was speaking of the physical wall built by Nehemiah and his followers.

Ezra is not speaking of his own day, but of Zerubbabel's day, when he talks of repairing the *ruins* of the Temple. The *us* refers to all Israelites, not just to his contemporaries.

According to verses 10-14, even after this act of grace on God's part, Israel has forsaken God's commandments again by intermarrying with *the people who practice these abominations.*

The Scripture passages referred to in verses 11-12 are not from *the prophets,* but from the Pentateuch. Perhaps Ezra mistakenly attributed these words to *the prophets,* or perhaps he considered Moses a prophet (see Deuteronomy 18:15, 18; 34:10; Hosea 12:13).

To eat the good of the land was to enjoy the best the land had to offer.

God . . . punished us less than our sins (NIV) *iniquities* (NRSV) deserved. Strict justice would have meant annihilation, for Israel was the people of a covenant. If the covenant were broken by one party, it could be discarded by the other.

Verses 13-14, while ostensibly addressed to God, were said more for the benefit of those who had gathered around Ezra.

The question posed in verse 14 is rhetorical. The answer is yes. It was a warning to those gathered around Ezra that God's judgment would strike again. Next time God's anger will destroy us so that there is no remnant or survivor.

The doxology with which Ezra closes his prayer (verse 15) is in reality a plea for God's grace. *We are before you in our guilt;* we are dependent upon thy grace.

The Response of the People (10:1-5)

At this point the Ezra memoirs come to a close. It is quite possible, however, that the information contained in chapter 10 was taken from the memoirs.

Ezra's prayer had precisely the effect on the people that he had wanted. They gathered to him, and *wept bitterly* with him.

There are three parts to Shecaniah's statement in verses 2-4: (1) We have broken faith with our God; (2) even now there is hope for Israel if we make a covenant with our God to send away all these wives or women and their children; (3) it is your duty, Ezra, to see that this is done; be strong and do it.

Shecaniah's words raise several questions. First, was Shecaniah's the only suggestion made? Who gave him the authority to speak for the community? Was he a recognized leader of the group? Second, had the solution proposed by Shecaniah been suggested by Ezra earlier? The words *according* (NIV) or *in accordance with* (NRSV) *to the counsel of my lord* certainly sound like it. And, if so, had it been prearranged that Shecaniah would make such a proposal? Third, on what basis did Shecaniah say to Ezra, *it is your duty* (NRSV) or as translated in the NIV: *This matter is in your hand* to do this? Was that one of the jobs Ezra was sent to Jerusalem to do? Or is this simply a recognition of Ezra as the leader of the people? We can only guess at the answers to all these questions.

Notice that Shecaniah's name is not among those listed as having married foreign women (verses 18-44). It is easy to make such a suggestion if you will not be affected by it. Some believe, however, that Shecaniah might have been the product of a mixed marriage, for he is the *son of Jehiel of the descendants of Elam*, and a Jehiel of the sons of Elam is listed as one of the offenders (10:26). Surely, however, these are different persons; for if not, Shecaniah would be advocating that he, his mother, and his brothers and sisters be ejected from the community. The meaning in verse 2b would then be, *There is hope for Israel* if you get rid of the likes of me. It is difficult to believe that is what Shecaniah meant.

The solution of Shecaniah is harsh. It would break up

EZRA, NEHEMIAH, AND ESTHER

families and ignore human love. It assumes *wives* (NRSV) or *women* and *children* can be *sent away* at will, as one might discard an old coat. True, the situation was perceived as desperate. And Shecaniah undoubtedly felt that desperate measures were called for. But we wonder whether a more humane solution to the problem could have been found than what Shecaniah here suggests.

Ezra responded by requiring that *priests and Levites and all Israel* take oath that they would do as had been said (verse 5).

Ezra's Proclamation and the Assembly (10:6-15)

Where the New Revised Standard Version has *spent the night*, the Hebrew and the NIV actually says "went." The NRSV has altered the text because (1) we have already been told that *Ezra . . . went to the room* (NIV) or *chamber of Jehohanan*; (2) it takes but a slight alteration of the Hebrew word to change "went" to *spent the night*; (3) the Septuagint translation of 1 Esdras 9:2 says "spent the night." "Went" makes perfectly good sense in the sentence, however.

Apparently the proclamation was made at the bidding of *the officials and . . . elders* rather than of Ezra. Anyone who did not show up within three days would have his property *forfeited* (literally, "devoted," that is, given to God) and he himself would be banned (literally, "separated") from the congregation. These were two of the powers given to Ezra by the king (see 7:26).

The open *square* (verse 9) was a large area in front of the Temple and was commonly used for mass meetings. The assembly was held *on the twentieth day* of Chislev, *the ninth month.* That corresponds roughly to the second week in December on our calendar, and was the season of the winter (or early) rains. The people, therefore, were *trembling,* (NRSV) or *greatly distressed* (NIV) not only because of the serious matter before them, but also because of the heavy rain.

The officials and the elders called the assembly (10:8),

but Ezra once again takes charge. He calls upon the guilty parties to *separate yourselves . . . from the foreign wives.*

In verses 12-25, the response of the people is amazing! We might have expected cries of protest, charges of "unfair," or at least sounds of weeping. Instead, the people say, it is so; *we must do as you have said.* The only concession they ask for is that Ezra not attempt to accomplish this work in one or two days. Only two persons, Jonathan and Jahzeiah, raise objection. It is not clear whether their objection is to Ezra's plan or to the people's timetable.

Meshullam and Shabethai support them, but again the meaning is not entirely clear. Do they support these two men, or do they support all the assembly? We cannot say for sure, but at most only four persons oppose Ezra's plan.

The Search and the Reform (10:16-44)

According to verses 16-17, the community followed the procedure suggested. The examination of each person from every city took three months.

A list of offenders is given in verses 18-44. The list begins with the priests who had married foreign women, moves then to *the Levites* and other Temple personnel, and finally lists the guilty laypersons.

They pledged themselves (NRSV) (verse 19) is literally *they gave their hands.* (NIV) This is a Hebrew idiom for taking an oath (see Ezekiel 17:18). The *guilt* offering, described in Leviticus 5:14-19, was an offering to atone for unwitting (unintentional) sin. Apparently, then, the returned exiles were unaware that to marry foreign women was contrary to God's law. It was to clarify such matters as this that Ezra came to teach the laws of God to those who did not know them (7:25).

The last half of verse 44 is unintelligible in the Hebrew. It reads, "and there were from them wives and they put children." The Revised Standard Version, therefore, follows 1 Esdras 9:36. The meaning, if not the wording, is clear: The reform was a success. The men put away their foreign wives and their children (verse 3).

EZRA, NEHEMIAH, AND ESTHER

§ § § § § § §

The Message of Ezra 9–10

When Ezra put his reform into effect, he faced the same problem we face when we try to take the Bible seriously. He was to see that the people obeyed the laws of God (7:26). Yet the law had been given centuries earlier. Could a law written for one age be valid in another?

The law said that the Israelites were not to intermarry with the Hittites, the Girgashites, the Amorites, the Canaanites, the Perizzites, the Hivites, and the Jebusites (Deuteronomy 7:1-2). But in Ezra's day these people were not the problem. Some of those nations no longer existed. The problem now lay with the Samaritans, the peoples of the land, those who worshiped God in the same manner in which the pagan gods were worshiped.

Was the law to be interpreted as being static? Was it to be carried out literally, with no room for interpretation? Or was the law flexible enough that it could be applied to a new situation? Ezra thought that it was. To the list of nations given in the law, he added the Ammonites, Moabites, and Egyptians (9:1).

Today we face the same question. How are we to interpret the Bible? Is the Bible a static book, to be followed literally, with no room for interpretation? If so, what do we do with such passages as Matthew 5:29-30 or Luke 14:26? Do we ignore them? Do we pretend Jesus never said them? Or can we follow the meaning and intent of the passage without obeying it literally?

There is no question about what Ezra would do: The spirit, not the letter, of the law must be carried out. Nor is there any question what Jesus would do. The law was not forever fixed. It could be, and should be, altered on occasion (see Matthew 5).

§ § § § § § §

Introduction to Nehemiah

Nehemiah, the Man

Nehemiah has not claimed the attention through the centuries that Ezra has. Yet he, too, was a towering figure of his day, and is mentioned in two books of the Apocrypha. In fact, when ben Sirach set out to "praise famous men," he mentioned the deeds of Nehemiah, but not those of Ezra (Ecclesiasticus 44:1; 49:13).

A story about Nehemiah not in the Protestant Bible is found in 2 Maccabees 1:18-36, and 2 Maccabees 2:13 says Nehemiah founded a library and collected the books about the kings, the prophets, and the writings of David. This undoubtedly is a reference to the books of Samuel, Kings, and Psalms. Just as Ezra was responsible for preserving the Law, Nehemiah preserved much of the rest of the Hebrew Bible. This is our only hint of such activity on the part of Nehemiah, however, and it is found in a book not considered to be historically reliable.

Like Ezra, Nehemiah has left us his memoirs, though scholars disagree on exactly how much and which portions of the book of Nehemiah come from Nehemiah himself. Nehemiah was a man of action, passionately devoted to living by the law of God. In the book that bears his name, we'll find Nehemiah building the city wall and putting into effect several religious reforms. In some ways he was a more likeable person than Ezra, but he, too, could be stern and demanding.

The Dates of Nehemiah and Ezra

The introduction to the book of Ezra states that one of
the problems of Old Testament scholarship is trying to
decide who returned to Jerusalem first—Ezra or
Nehemiah. Probably Nehemiah did, and reasons for this
are given in the introduction to Ezra. It was also stated
there that archaeological evidence supported this claim.
Here is that evidence.

In the fifth century B.C., there was a Jewish community
on Elephantine Island in Egypt. Among the materials
found there, left by this community, was a letter dated in
the seventeenth year of Darius II, which would be 407 B.C.
The letter is addressed to Delaiah and Shelemiah, sons of
Sanballat, whom the letter identifies as the governor of
Samaria. Since the letter was sent to the governor's sons,
it is reasonable to assume that Sanballat was getting up
in years, and had turned over to his sons the
responsibility of governing the land.

This fits well with our belief that Nehemiah came to
Jerusalem in 445 B.C., the twentieth year of Artaxerxes I
(see Nehemiah 1:1; 2:1). For, one of Nehemiah's most
persistent foes was named Sanballat. And although
Nehemiah never refers to him as governor, it is obvious
that Sanballat was in a position of authority. He was a
young and vigorous leader when Nehemiah was there.

Thirty-eight years later, in 407 (when the Elephantine
letter was written), Sanballat was too old to govern, but
kept the title of governor, and ruled through his sons.

The same letter refers to Jehohanan as the high priest
at the time of the destruction of the Elephantine temple
in 410 B.C. That information fits well with our belief that
Ezra returned to Jerusalem, not in the seventh year of
Artaxerxes I, but in the seventh year of Artaxerxes II, that
is, in 397 B.C. For, Ezra 10:6 indicates that Ezra went to
the chamber of Jehohanan, the son of Eliashib, where he
spent the night. Now, Eliashib was the high priest in
445 B.C., during the time of Nehemiah (Nehemiah 3:1, 20).

If he had become high priest at a young age, he could have continued in that post for another thirty years or so. Then Jehohanan, his son, could have become high priest, and would have been in office at the time of the destruction of the Elephantine temple in 410 and when Ezra arrived in Jerusalem in 397. Thus the archaeological evidence fits the theory that Nehemiah preceded Ezra in returning to Jerusalem. At the same time, it destroys the contrary theory that Ezra returned first.

What leaves the question open, however, is the fact that archaeology is not infallible. Whereas the evidence cited above would support the conclusions to which we have come, other archaeological evidence indicates that there was a second Sanballat, who served as governor of Samaria during the reign of Artaxerxes II. If these are the Sanballat and the Artaxerxes referred to in the Book of Nehemiah, then Nehemiah came to Jerusalem, not in 445, but in 384. And that reopens the possibility that Ezra preceded Nehemiah. It seems best, until more definite information can be obtained, to stay with the earlier dates.

Nehemiah 1–2

Introduction to These Chapters

Approximately one-fourth of the books of the Bible begin with a title. Nehemiah is one of these books (see Nehemiah 1:1). Some have wondered at this, since Nehemiah was originally not a separate book, but a part of the book of Ezra (see Introduction to Ezra). This need not puzzle us, however, since other books of the Old Testament have titles to sections within the books (see Isaiah 2:1; 13:1; 15:1; Jeremiah 21:1; 25:1; and many other places). These titles within books simply mean that the compiler of the book—in this case, the Chronicler—is now introducing into his work some material from a different source. The memoirs of Nehemiah begin at 1:1 and continue through 7:5, excluding, perhaps, the list of workers in chapter 3.

Here is an outline of Nehemiah 1–2.
I.   Nehemiah Hears Distressing News (1:1-11a)
II. Permission to Go to Jerusalem (1:11b–2:8)
III. Nehemiah Challenges the People (2:9-20)
    A. The arrival and inspection (2:9-16)
    B. The challenge and responses (2:17-20)

Nehemiah Hears Distressing News (1:1-11a)

Nothing is known of *Hacaliah*. He is mentioned only here and in 10:1.

In the twentieth year undoubtedly refers to the twentieth year of Artaxerxes the king. As we shall see in 2:1, however, there is some confusion about the year.

Susa was the winter capital of the Persian kings (see the commentary on Ezra 6:2).

Who was *Hanani* (verse 2), and where did he live? Was he a blood brother to Nehemiah? Some have thought so, on the basis of 7:2. Here, however, he is simply called *one of my brothers*. Where did Hanani live? Did he, too, come from Judah to see Nehemiah? Or did the men from Judah come to Susa, meet there with Hanani, and then go to see Nehemiah? We cannot be sure, but the latter possibility seems more likely.

To what great catastrophe do the men of Judah refer in verse 3? Jerusalem had been destroyed by the Babylonians in 587, and this could be the devastation referred to here. But that had happened 142 years earlier! It is difficult to see why that fact, already known by every Jew, would bring such a reaction from Nehemiah (verse 4). Surely their reference is to some more recent event.

In Ezra 4:7-23, we have the one and only reference in the book of Ezra to the days of Artaxerxes. There, Rehum sent a letter to Artaxerxes indicating that the rebellious Jews were rebuilding Jerusalem's walls. Artaxerxes' reply was a command that the men *be made to cease* such activity until a further decree was made. Then we read that Rehum and his associates went to Jerusalem and by force and power made them cease. It is reasonable to assume that Rehum not only made them stop building, but also destroyed the work the Jews had already done. If so, it is very likely that this is the news which the men of Judah brought to Nehemiah.

Nehemiah's prayer in verses 5-11 reminds us of Ezra's prayer. Both men confess the sins of the people, both now and in the past. Both identify with the guilty. Both acknowledge that God gave the people plenty of warning, and that the people's punishment had been just. Both acknowledge God's grace in dealing with the people in the past, and both plead for God's mercy in the present situation. These similarities have caused many to wonder if these prayers were not composed by the Chronicler rather than their being verbatim reports of the prayers of Ezra and Nehemiah.

In speaking of the sins of Judah, Nehemiah says, I and my father's or family's house have sinned (verse 6). Some have seen this as an indication that Nehemiah was of royal blood, for it was commonplace to refer to a king's country as his *house*.

The words and give success to your servant today, and grant him mercy or favor in the presence of this man (verse 11) seem out of place in this prayer. The prayer is complete without them, and a new topic is introduced with them. *This man* is left unidentified (until the next chapter), and the ordeal for which Nehemiah wished success did not come that day, but four months later. For more on this, see 2:4.

Permission to Go to Jerusalem (1:11*b*–2:8)

The position of *cupbearer to the king* was much more important than the title seems to imply. The cupbearer was the king's personal valet. He set the table, poured the wine, and tasted the food. Often the cupbearer was a constant companion and trusted friend of the king. Tobit tells us that Ahikar, cupbearer in the days of King Esarhaddon, was second in command in the kingdom (Tobit 1:22).

Four months have now passed. *Kislev* (NIV) or *Chislev* (NRSV) (1:1) is the ninth month; Nisan is the first. Notice, however, that in both 1:2 and 2:1, the year is given as *the twentieth year of King Artaxerxes*. That is impossible, since the events of 1:1ff. happened before the events of 2:1 and following. Some, therefore, believe 1:1 should read, "the nineteenth year." Another solution would be to say that Nehemiah was using the Syrian calendar, which began in the fall, rather than either the Jewish or Persian calendars, both of which began in the spring. However, this suggestion hardly seems likely.

Nehemiah thought he had successfully hidden his *sadness*, but he could not fool the king. Nehemiah was then *very much afraid*. This fear was, perhaps, for two reasons. First, Nehemiah was nervous. He had been waiting for this opportunity for four months, and now it was here. He knew that at that moment, the fate of Jerusalem rested upon him. But secondly, Nehemiah was afraid because he knew that earlier, Artaxerxes had ordered that the building on the Jerusalem wall be stopped. What Nehemiah was about to do was to ask the king to revoke the order he had given earlier (see Ezra 4:7-16 and the commentary on Nehemiah 1:3).

Notice that Nehemiah never mentioned Jerusalem by name. Nor did he reveal that his desire was to rebuild the city wall. These disclosures must come, but first it was important to gain the king's sympathy. So Nehemiah spoke in terms of *the place where my fathers' are buried* (NIV) or *to the city of my ancestors' grave* (NRSV) (verse 3). Anyone could understand his desire to maintain the sacredness and dignity of his ancestors' graves.

The place of where the ancestors are buried once again raises the question of whether Nehemiah was of royal blood, for all the former kings of Judah were buried in Jerusalem. This allows for Nehemiah to be a descendant of David, but it does not prove this relationship, for other families were buried there, too.

Following the king's question, Nehemiah *prayed to the God of heaven* (verse 4). But what did he say in that prayer? We are not told. It could have been only a very brief prayer, for the king was waiting for an answer. The prayer that seemed so out of place tacked onto the end of the prayer of 1:5-11 fits perfectly here (see the commentary on 1:11*a*). Possibly this prayer was preserved, and was erroneously attached to the longer prayer in chapter 1.

The words, *the queen sitting beside him* (verse 6) have caused a great deal of discussion. Why was this fact mentioned? Does it imply that the queen looked favorably upon Nehemiah's request? Or that Artaxerxes responded differently when the queen was with him? Does it imply that there is a time gap between verse 1 and verse 6, the former being at a banquet, the latter when the king was dining with the queen? We can only guess at the answers to these questions.

The mention of the queen also raises another question. The general practice of the times was to make eunuchs of all male servants who were allowed access to the queen. Was Nehemiah, then, a eunuch? Or had he, for some unknown reason, been spared this custom? We cannot say for sure, but the issues will arise again in Chapter 6.

The discourse recorded in verses 6-8 is an abbreviated report of what may have taken place during several conversations.

Like Ezra, Nehemiah attributes his good fortune in dealing with the king to the fact that *the gracious hand of my God was upon me.*

Perhaps the Temple had a special *fortress*, or perhaps Nehemiah means *the fortress* (NRSV) or *gates* (NIV) which guarded the city. If so, it may be the same as the Tower of Hananel in 3:1. Also, it may be the predecessor of the Tower (or Fortress) of Antonia, built by Herod, perhaps on the same spot.

Had *the residence* (NIV) or *house which I will occupy* (NRSV) already been selected? And, if so, was it the governor's mansion? Was Nehemiah sent to Jerusalem as governor, or was he so appointed after he arrived? The former possibility is the more likely. Probably, therefore, the house was, indeed, the governor's home.

The Arrival and Inspection (2:9-16)

Unlike Ezra, Nehemiah had military protection for his journey.

Sanballat was governor of Samaria (see the Introduction to Nehemiah, pages 54-56. It is not clear what the term *the Horonite* means. Perhaps it designates his birthplace (Beth-horon or Horonaim). Or maybe it identifies him as a worshiper of the pagan god Horon (although both his sons had names compounded with "Yahweh," the name of the Israelite God, and one of his daughters married into the family of the high priest; see 13:28). Most commentators see *the Horonite* as a derogatory term, but we cannot be sure of its meaning.

Whose servant was Tobiah? Some have thought he was Sanballat's servant. More likely, however, he was the king's servant, that is, a high-ranking official. If so, he would be called *the Ammonite* to delineate the area of his rule.

Sanballat and Tobiah would be displeased that Nehemiah had come to seek the welfare of the people of Israel because that would mean less power for them.

Note again the similarity between the stories of Ezra and Nehemiah (Ezra 8:32). See also Joshua 3:1-2. Perhaps *three days* was a customary waiting period after a long journey.

It was important for Nehemiah to keep the purpose of his trip to Jerusalem a secret until he was ready to act, for he knew of the opposition of Sanballat and Tobiah, and he was not sure yet who in the city would be loyal to which side. So he took with him only *a few men* whom he could trust, and only one *moum* (NIV) or *animal* (NRSV) so as to not arouse attention.

According to verses 13-15, Nehemiah left by *the Valley Gate* on the western wall, and moved around the wall in a counter-clockwise direction until he reached *the King's Pool*. Then, he turned back, retraced his steps, and re-entered the city by the same gate. All this he did *by night*.

This is the only place in the Bible where *the Jackal's Well* (NIV) or *the dragon spring* (NRSV) is mentioned. This is also the only mention of *the king's pool*, though the Pool of Shelah (3:15) is undoubtedly the same body of water.

In verse 16, the secret nature of Nehemiah's inspection is once again emphasized.

The Challenge and Responses (2:17-20)

Nehemiah's challenge to the people is three-pronged: *Jerusalem* is in *disgrace*; God has blessed me in this; the king has sent me here to do this. The response of the people was immediate: *Let us start building*.

According to verse 19, the response of Nehemiah's enemies was not long in coming. *Geshem the Arab* is now mentioned along with Sanballat and Tobiah. From non-biblical sources we learn that Geshem ruled a large area, including northern Arabia, as far north as Moab, and stretching westward across the Negeb all the way to Egypt. Their attack on Nehemiah was twofold—derision and accusation. Their questions were implied threats. The king shall be told you are *rebelling against* him.

To have *no share . . . in Jerusalem* (verse 20) is to own no land there and be no part of the community there. To have *no claim* is to have no authority. To have no *historic right* is to have no heirs, no work to be remembered by, no one to mourn when you die. What Nehemiah was saying, then, was, "You have no business here because you are not one of us, your authority stops at the district line, and once we get this wall built, even the memory of you will fade from existence." Nehemiah was determined that nothing would keep him from accomplishing the great work before him.

§ § § § § § §

The Message of Nehemiah 1–2

Nehemiah had a multi-faceted personality. Many of his traits are worthy of emulation.

§ He was a man of feelings, and he was not afraid to express them. When told of the plight of Jerusalem and the people there, he wept for days (see 1:4).

§ He was a man of prayer. He fasted and prayed, and laid his concerns before God (1:4-11; 2:4).

§ He was a man of confession. When detailing the sins of his people, he included himself as one of the sinners (1:6-7).

§ He was a man of spiritual discipline. His prayer in Chapter 1 shows an intimate knowledge of the books of Moses. He obviously read them frequently (1:7-10).

§ He was a man of courage. He was afraid when questioned by Artaxerxes, but he did not let his fear keep him from doing what he knew he must (2:2-3). Nor did he let the threats of Sanballat, Tobiah, and Geshem keep him from building the wall (2:19-20).

§ He was a man of wisdom. He knew what to say in order to get the desired results (2:5 with the king; 2:17-18 with the people of Jerusalem).

§ He was a man of faith. He knew that his success was due to God (2:8, 18, 20).

§ He was a man of action. He gathered the facts first (2:12-15), but then was ready to go to work to get the job done (2:17-18, 20).

§ § § § § § §

Nehemiah 3–4

Introduction to These Chapters

In these two chapters we'll see a determined Nehemiah organizing his people, beginning the work he came to do, and defending his efforts against those who opposed him. Equally as determined, yet doomed to failure, are those who try to frustrate Nehemiah's work.

Here is an outline of these chapters.

I. The Work Begins (3:1-32)

II. Opposition and Countermeasures (4:1-23)

The Work Begins (3:1-32)

In a sense the material of chapter 3 is appropriately placed. We have just finished reading of Nehemiah's determination to rebuild the wall, and here we are given the details of that work. On the other hand, the long list of who worked where on the wall is an obvious interruption of the story. Furthermore, the details of chapter 3 do not always fit well with what we read in other portions of Nehemiah's book (see on verse 3, for example). For that reason, some scholars see chapter 3 as having been misplaced from a later section of Nehemiah's memoirs, while other scholars regard chapter 3 as not a part of Nehemiah's memoirs at all.

It was unusual for the high priest to engage in manual labor. It is a tribute to Eliashib, and also to Nehemiah, that he was willing, or was persuaded, to do so. The section of wall built by the priests is the only section which was consecrated prior to the completion of the entire wall. Perhaps this was because the sacrificial animals were brought into the city through *the Sheep Gate*. With only a slight emendation, the text may read, *they set the beams in it*, rather than *they dedicated* (NIV) or *consecrated it*. (NRSV) Though some scholars prefer this reading, it seems best to leave the text as it stands.

Strangely, the wall seems to be at a later stage of repair in verse 3 than at 6:1, for there the doors had not been set in the gates. Here, however, the doors in the Fish Gate were set, along with its bars, cross pieces to secure the door, and its bolts, perhaps hinges or perhaps latches for the cross bars.

Meremoth (verse 4) is of the lineage of *Hakkoz*, whose descendants were among those barred from the priesthood because they could not prove their ancestry. Here Meremoth, apparently a very young man, is not a priest, for the priests have already been mentioned (verse 1). Forty-eight years later, however, at the time of Ezra, Meremoth was a highly respected priest. (See the commentary on Ezra 8:33-34.)

The wall is said to have been repaired here, whereas it was built in verses 1-3. That is, perhaps, to be expected, since the sections of the wall mentioned in verses 1-3 were on the north side of the city, the side reached first by Nebuchadnezzar's troops, and the only side of the city not protected by valleys. The word *repairs* is used for all the rest of the wall, with three exceptions. Two gates are said to have been rebuilt (verses 13, 14), and the wall of the Pool of Shelah is said to have been built (verse 15).

We are not told why the *nobles* of Tekoa did not assist in the building of the wall (verse 5). Three facts may have had a bearing on it, however. First, no men from Tekoa are listed as having returned from exile, either with Zerubbabel or with Ezra. Secondly, Tekoa was some ten miles south of Jerusalem; a wall around Jerusalem, therefore, would not be of any value to the people of

Tekoa. And third, Tekoa was somewhat isolated, making it more susceptible to attacks of retaliation from the armies of Geshem. None of this, however, prevented the citizens of Tekoa from repairing two sections of the wall (see verse 27).

Who were under the jurisdiction of the governor (verse 7) is literally, *to the seat of the governor.* If *seat* is taken metaphorically, meaning authority, then the NRSV is accurate. Many believe, however, that the word refers to the governor's chair, comparable, perhaps, to the throne of a king. In that case, the governor would have had a residence in Jerusalem.

Harhaiah is unknown as a name except here in verse 8. A slight emendation of the text would yield *guild.* The meaning would then be that *Uzziel* belonged to the guild of the *goldsmiths.*

The Broad Wall may have been a section of the wall that had been reinforced at some time in the past.

Rephaiah and Shallum (verse 12) were each ruler of half the district of Jerusalem. Probably, however, the district of Jerusalem included territory outside the city as well as within it, as the alternate reading of the Revised Standard Version indicates.

Another section (verse 11) is literally *a second section.* We have not been told of the first section repaired by *Malchijah . . . and Hasshub.* This is one of several indications that our list of workers and places they repaired is incomplete.

The Tower of the Ovens is unknown except for here and 12:38. Perhaps, however, the bakers' street referred to in Jeremiah 37:21 led to or passed by *the tower.*

Shallum is the only person of whom it is said that his daughters helped in making the repairs (see verse 12). Since Shallum was ruler of half the district, and since towns under one's rule are spoken of as *his daughters,* some believe that is the meaning here. There is no reason, however, why *daughters* cannot be taken literally.

Still debated among Old Testament scholars is the question of how large Nehemiah's city was (see verse 13). If it included the Western Hill, then the valley into which *the Valley Gate* opened was the northern end of the Valley of Hinnom. If, however, the city was confined to the Eastern Hill, the gate opened into the Tyropoean Valley, which separated the Eastern Hill from the Western. The Valley of Hinnom is mentioned frequently in the Bible; the Tyropoean Valley is never spoken of by name.

According to verse 14, once again the wall is at a later stage of repair than at 6:1 (see on 3:3).

The Fountain Gate (verse 15) is the only gate that is said to have been covered.

The Pool of Shelah (NRSV) may be the same as the King's Pool (2:14), and perhaps is identical with the *Pool of Siloam* (NIV) to which Jesus sent the man born blind (John 9:7).

The king's garden is also mentioned in 2 Kings 25:4 and Jeremiah 39:4; 52:7. It may be identical to the garden of Uzza (2 Kings 21:18, 26).

The Nehemiah referred to in verse 16 is, of course, a different Nehemiah.

For the *tombs* (NIV) or *graves* (NRSV) of David, see the commentary on 2:3.

The house of the warriors (NRSV) or *hernes* (NIV) was built originally for David's mighty men (mentioned in 2 Samuel 23:8-39 and several other places). The house probably was used thereafter as a military barracks.

For a discussion of the name *Binnui* (found in verse 18), see on verse 24.

The Angle (verse 19) was probably a sharp curve in the wall, which is distinct from *the corner* in verses 24-25.

The priests from the surrounding area mentioned in verse 22 were probably those who lived in the rural areas of the Jerusalem district (see the commentary on 3:9).

In verse 18, Bavvai is said to be *the son of Henadad*. Here in verse 24, *Bennui* is. That in itself is not enough to raise our suspicions. But the name *Bavvai* is unknown except for the one mention of it in verse 18. Furthermore, we are told here that *Bennui . . . repaired another section*, implying that he had repaired one already. All these facts together lead many to the conclusion that *Bavvai* in verse 18 should read *Bennui*.

Either not all the Temple servants mentioned in verse 26 lived *on Ophel*, or the house of the temple servants mentioned in verse 31 was a temporary residence for them as they performed their duties.

The phrase *the sixth son of* (verse 30) is unusual, and we do not know why this piece of information is given here, but nowhere else. Some suspect a scribal error.

With verse 32, the circuit is now complete.

Opposition and Countermeasures (4:1-23)

The story left hanging at 2:20 is now resumed. Chapter 2 closed with Sanballat, Tobiah, and Geshem deriding the Jews, and asking, *What is this thing that you are doing?* Nehemiah responded with a prayer. Chapter 4 begins in exactly the same way. Sanballat and Tobiah are ridiculing the Jews; Sanballat asks, *What are these feeble Jews doing?* and Nehemiah responds with a prayer.

In the Hebrew Bible, the first six verses of chapter 4 are verses 33-38 of chapter 3.

Sanballat's series of five questions in verse 2 are contemptuous in nature. *Will they restore things?* (NRSV) or *the walls* (NIV) The emphasis is upon *they*. This was a job for professional builders. Do they think just anybody can *restore* a wall? *Will they finish in a day?* That is, *these feeble Jews* don't have any idea what a monumental task they have taken upon themselves. *Will they revive the stones out of the heaps of rubbish, and burned ones at that?* (NIV or as in the NIV: *can they bring the stones back to life from those heaps of rubble—burned as they are?* Do they expect to *restore* a wall with those? Sanballat was correct in saying the Jews had a hard task before them. He was wrong in saying they couldn't do it. The wall they built protected the city for more than a century.

In verses 4-5, Nehemiah responded to these taunts by

praying. Sensitive people often have been offended by this prayer. We cannot deny that it is vindictive in nature. Yet Nehemiah was convinced that he was doing the job that God wanted done. To oppose the work he was doing, therefore, was to oppose the will of God. That is why Nehemiah could say, they have thrown insults in the face of the builders. For similar prayers in the Old Testament, see Psalms 79:12; 109:6-20; 139:21-22; Jeremiah 18:21-22. For a New Testament example see Luke 9:51-56.

To half its height (verse 6) is literally, "to its middle." The New Revised Standard Version and NIV is probably correct in interpreting this to mean *to half its height*.

There are two new developments in verses 7-8. First, *Sanballat and Tobiah and the Arabs* (the forces of Geshem) are joined by the Ammonites and the Ashdodites. Samaria, Sanballat's territory, lay to the north; Ammon, Tobiah's territory, lay to the east; Geshem's territory lay to the south; and the territory of the Ashdodites included all the land of the former Philistines, and lay to the west. Judah was now completely surrounded by enemies.

Secondly, for the first time, violence is threatened. Until now Sanballat and Tobiah had used scorn and ridicule as their weapons. That had not worked. Now they *plotted together* with all the surrounding nations *to come and fight against Jerusalem.*

Once again in time of crisis, Nehemiah turned to prayer. In addition, however, he set a guard as a protection against them day and night.

Who was *Judah*, mentioned in verse 10? Was that a person, or did the author intend us to understand that all the people were becoming disheartened and not able to work on the wall? Probably the latter. These were discouraging times, indeed.

According to verses 11-12, the enemies planned a surprise attack. But *the Jews who lived near*, that is, who lived outside of Jerusalem in the surrounding territory, warned Nehemiah of the planned attack. *Ten times* simply means many times, over and over again.

The meaning of verses 13-14 seems to be that

Nehemiah gathered his people, either at the places where the city would be most vulnerable to attack, or at those places where the people would be most visible to the enemy—in open places where the wall was lowest. That would be a way of saying to Sanballat and the others, "We know you are coming, and we are ready!" It also would be a show of strength for the people of Judah, to give them courage and determination. Nehemiah issued a threefold challenge to the people—*do not be afraid . . . remember the* LORD *. . .* and fight for your brothers (NIV) or *kin* (NRSV) *your sons, your daughters, your wives, and your homes.*

According to verse 15, the strategy worked! The enemies learned that *God had frustrated* their plan to make a surprise attack; and the people of Judah left behind them their fear and discouragement (verse 10), and all *returned to the wall,* each to his work.

In verses 16-23, we read that Nehemiah continued to take precautions. It is not clear who Nehemiah's *servants* (NRSV) or *men* (NIV) were. They are to be distinguished from both the leaders, who stood behind, and *the house of Judah,* who were building on the wall. Nehemiah refers to his servants in 4:16, 22; 5:10, 16; and 13:19.

Some of the measures taken by Nehemiah seem impractical. For one to carry with one hand a crate of stones, and with the other a weapon is cumbersome at best. And for there to be only one who sounded the trumpet would hardly provide security for people separated on the wall. One cannot miss the main point, however, that the needed precautions were taken even as work on the wall continued.

The last words of chapter 4, *each kept his weapon in his right hand* (NRSV) or as translated in the NIV—*each had his weapon even when he went for water,* bear little relation to what the Hebrew actually says. This translation is an attempt to make sense out of an unintelligible text. What the Hebrew actually says is, "each his weapon the water." We cannot explain how the text came to be so badly corrupted at this point.

§ § § § § § §

The Message of Nehemiah 3–4

§ Perhaps the greatest lesson to be learned from these chapters is the interlocking nature of faith and works. No one was more convinced than Nehemiah that the good hand of the Lord was upon God's people. Yet, though *we prayed to our God*, Nehemiah also set up a guard as a protection . . . day and night (4:9). And though Nehemiah knew *our God will fight for us* (4:20), he also took precautions to make sure the work got done and his people were protected. He was a man of faith; but he was also a man of action.

§ Another lesson we need to learn is how to come together as one. When the wall needed rebuilding, it was not just the common people who came to work. All the people of Judah came, regardless of status, regardless of position. Priests and Levites, goldsmiths and servants, rich and poor labored side by side. And though some internal problems appeared later, there is no hint of them here. The people were one. They believed God was calling upon them to do this great work, and they were determined to do it.

§ § § § § § §

Nehemiah 5

Introduction to These Chapters

Once again we come to a section of material that is out of chronological sequence. In the first place, it is inconceivable that Nehemiah would stop to have a *great assembly* (NRSV) or *large meeting* (NIV) (5:7) of his people in the midst of the tense situation described in chapter 4. Second, chapter 5 seems to be an insertion, for the story left hanging at the end of chapter 4 is picked up again in chapter 6. Third, neither Sanballat nor any other adversary is mentioned in chapter 5. The situation described here seems to come from a time when Sanballat is no longer a threat. Fourth, the famine and the sins resulting from it tie in well with the situation described in chapter 13, during Nehemiah's second stint as governor of Judah. And finally, it is evident from 5:14 that the entire episode comes from Nehemiah's second term, for the entire twelve years of his first term as governor are spoken of in the past tense.

Probably the Chronicler chose to relate this story here because it suited his purposes. He is showing the difficulties encountered by the restored community. So far he has emphasized problems from without. Now he wants to show that Nehemiah had internal problems, too.

Here is an outline of chapter 5.

I. An Internal Problem (5:1-5)
II. Nehemiah Acts; the People Respond (5:6-13)
III. Nehemiah's Unselfishness as Governor (5:14-19)

An Internal Problem (5:1-5)

The word translated *outcry* in verse 1 implies dire circumstances. It was used by the people of Israel when Pharaoh's army pursued them at the time of the Exodus (Exodus 14:10). It was also used in the law to define whether a woman had been raped or had consented to the relationship (Deuteronomy 22:23-27).

It is rare in the Bible for women to lodge cries of protest. The fact that the wives did so in this instance is an indication of the severity of the crisis.

The people were experiencing three different levels of adversity. These are listed in order in verses 2-4, beginning with the most severe. As verse 2 now stands, the first problem is simply too many people for the amount of available food. With only a small change in the Hebrew, however, the verse reads *our sons and our daughters are given in pledge*. That is, the poorest people, unable to pay their debts, and having no property to sell, had been forced to hire out their children as indentured servants until the debt was paid. That this was the original meaning is shown by verse 5, we are forcing our sons and daughters to be slaves. This arrangement was permitted by law (Exodus 21:7), and had been practiced in pre-exilic Israel (2 Kings 4:1).

A second group, more fortunate than the first, were those who owned land, and therefore did not have to sell their children as slaves. However, they did have to mortgage their fields, their vineyards, and their houses to *get grain because of the famine*. The one who mortgaged his fields and vineyards would continue to work the land, but all the profits from the crops belonged to the creditor until the debt was paid in full. This, of course, drove the person deeper into debt, and it was only a matter of time before he would join those in the first category.

The third group, the most fortunate of the poor, escaped having to mortgage their property, but had to borrow in order to pay the taxes on it (verse 4). Any time one borrowed, however, a "pledge," or what we could call "collateral," was required (Deuteronomy 24:10-11). A

EZRA, NEHEMIAH, AND ESTHER

small pledge was required for a small loan, a larger pledge for a larger loan. Anyone who had to borrow, therefore, might eventually end up among those who had to mortgage their entire estate.

The king's tax was a graduated tax. Beginning with Darius, the fields and vineyards were taxed according to their yield the preceding year. The better the yield, the more the tax the following year.

The meaning of the first part of verse 5 is not, "our children are as good as their children," but rather, "we and our children are of the same flesh and blood, the same race, as they and their children are." Their cry is, "Our own brethren are doing this to us!"

Special mention is made of the daughters for two reasons. First, sons were given into slavery before daughters were. To say that *some of our daughters have already been enslaved* (NIV) or *ravished* (NIV), then, is to say that we are just about to the end of our rope. Second, women taken in pledge often were treated as concubines. This, in fact, was a major reason why even the youngest of the sons was indentured before any of the daughters were.

Nehemiah Acts; the People Respond (5:6-13)

The law forbade charging interest to an Israelite (Leviticus 25:35-37). It was on this basis that Nehemiah *brought charges against (NRSV)* or *accused* (NIV) the nobles and the officials. For the maximum effect, he brought the charges before a great assembly, that is, in front of the entire community.

In verse 9 Nehemiah mentions yet another reason for correcting the injustice—*to prevent the taunts of the nations our enemies.* (NRSV) or as translated in the NIV *to avoid the reproach of our gentle enemies.* They had enough problems with their neighbors without adding this to them!

Verse 10 catches us by surprise, for it seems to say that Nehemiah and his *brothers* were as guilty as anyone else. They, too, were lending money and grain to the poor.

There is nothing wrong, however, with lending money to the poor. And it is possible that the words *let us stop this taking of interest* (NRSV) or in the NIV *but let the exacting of usury stop!* do not mean that Nehemiah had been charging interest, but that he was saying, "You should not charge interest to your fellow Jews, even as I don't."

The Israelites had provisions in their laws that sought to protect the poor. One of these said that every seven years the people of Israel were to release their fellow Israelites from any debts owed them (Deuteronomy 15:1-2). Nehemiah, however, challenges the creditors to make such remission immediately, *this very day* (NRSV) or immediately (NRSV) (verse 11).

The phrase *the hundredth of* (NIV) implied in the NRSV by the word *interest* is puzzling because that is extremely low interest. Some have suggested that a *hundredth* per month is meant, but even that is only 12 per cent, small by the standards of the day. With only a small emendation of the Hebrew text, *the hundredth of* becomes *the pledge of*, and that makes much better sense. What Nehemiah, then, is telling the nobles to do is to return the items they had taken in pledge.

To take an oath before the priests (verse 12) was the ancient equivalent of swearing on the Bible. For other ancient methods, see Genesis 24:9 and Ruth 4:7.

The ancient prophet often underscored his message by dramatizing the curse that would be upon the people if they ignored his words. In verse 13, Nehemiah was reviving that old custom.

The word *amen* is a transliteration from the Hebrew. The word means *so be it* or *let it be so.*

Nehemiah's Unselfishness as Governor (5:14-19)

Nehemiah recalls for his readers his own unselfishness and generosity during his years as governor of Judah. He is contrasting his actions with those of the nobles and officials just discussed.

It is not clear who Nehemiah means by *the former* (NRSV) or *earlier* (NIV) *governors* mentioned in verse 15.

We know of Sheshbazzar (Ezra 5:14) and Zerubbabel (Haggai 1:1, 14; 2:2, 21). Perhaps there been others as well, but if so, we have no record of them. The impression left is that Nehemiah is speaking of more recent governors than Shesbazzar and Zerubbabel. Possibly the former governors were Samaritan governors. Judah could have been a part of the Samaritan district before Artaxerxes sent Nehemiah to be governor of Judah. If so, that would further explain Sanballat's hostility toward Nehemiah.

Their assistants (NIV) or *servants* refers to the governor's minor officials.

Nehemiah is not listed in chapter 3 as having worked on the wall. Chapter 4 gives us reason to think he did (see 4:15 and 4:21, where the "we" is used). It would still be possible, however, to see Nehemiah's role as organizing the project, overseeing the work, and inspiring the people. But here in 5:16, it once again sounds as if Nehemiah did actual manual labor on this wall. Furthermore, Nehemiah's servants worked on the wall, and he acquired no land while he was governor. In all of these ways, he served the people well.

This verse gives us our only hint concerning where Nehemiah was when he wrote his memoirs. When he refers to the wall of Jerusalem as *this wall*, he sounds physically close to it. Probably, then, he was in Jerusalem when he wrote these words.

As governor of Judah, Nehemiah was expected to feed the officials in his own district and any *from the nations. . . around us* when they stopped in with the caravans which accompanied them. The amount of food required for one day is staggering! Even so, Nehemiah did not demand the food allowance.

In verse 13, Nehemiah prays a characteristic prayer. He asks for divine reward for his generosity and unselfishness. Some criticize Nehemiah for his self-congratulatory prayers, but in view of the avarice generally displayed by high-ranking government officials—both then and now—he deserves special recognition.

The Message of Nehemiah 5

§ As we read the opening verses of chapter 5, our sympathies are drawn instinctively to the poor. Their land is being wrested from them, and their families are being torn asunder by the merciless policies of the nobles and officials. We applaud the quick and decisive actions which Nehemiah took to correct the situation.

However, Nehemiah's policies cannot be applied universally. The rich would not loan their money at all if they could not require collateral and charge interest. Especially would they not loan their money if they were then expected to cancel the debts of the borrowers. The poor, therefore, rather than being helped by Nehemiah's policies, would remain forever in poverty.

Extraordinary circumstances require extraordinary measures. The difficulty is to know when the old is no longer usable, and what is needed to replace it. The one who is able to discern these things, and to convince others to try the new, is the one we refer to as a leader.

§ In chapter 4, the people of Israel were united. Together they determined to build the wall regardless of the jeers and threats of Sanballat. They gave it their all; they did what was necessary; they got the job done. But in chapter 5 there is no longer unity. Instead, there is division, bickering, and exploitation of one another. Instead of fighting a common foe, they were fighting one another. Had it not been for Nehemiah and the strong leadership he exerted, everything the people of God stood for might have been lost. A community can cope with external threats; it may even be made stronger because of them. But let the people begin to fight among themselves, and the battle is lost.

§ § § § § § §

Nehemiah 6–7

Introduction to These Chapters

Chapter 6 resumes the story of chapter 4. Some lapse of time is evident, however. Chapter 4 ends with the builders sleeping with their clothes on in order to be ready for either work or battle, whereas chapter 6 begins with the wall completed except for putting the doors in the gates. Nehemiah's enemies make their final attempts to prevent the finishing of the wall, but again they fail, and the wall is completed.

In chapter 7, Nehemiah's concern is to populate the city now that the wall is finished. Here is an outline of these chapters.

I. Plots Against Nehemiah's Life (6:1-14)
   A. "Let us meet together" (6:1-4)
   B. "It is reported . . ." (6:5-9)
   C. "They are coming to kill you" (6:10-14)
II. The Walls Are Completed (6:15-19)
III. Getting Started in Jerusalem (7:1-73)
   A. Leaders appointed and people counted (7:1-69)
   B. The people settle in their towns (7:70-73)

"Let Us Meet Together" (6:1-4)

In verse 1 we read that the doors had not been set in the gates. Earlier (3:3, 6, 13–15) we had been told that certain gates had been repaired and their doors set. Probably the description in chapter 3 is later than the narrative of chapter 6.

In verse 2, Sanballat and Gesham propose a meeting between Nehemiah and themselves. Apparently they pretended to come in reconciliation, but Nehemiah discerned that they intended to do him harm.

The *plain of Ono* was about fifteen miles northwest of Jerusalem, outside of Nehemiah's jurisdiction. Nehemiah would have been a prime target for any kind of ambush Sanballat might have set for him there.

It is ironic that Nehemiah used as his excuse for not meeting with them the very work they were attempting to stop (verse 3).

"It Is Reported . . ." (6:5-9)

According to verses 5-8, after four attempts to lure Nehemiah away, Sanballat changed his tactics. He sent his servant to Nehemiah with a letter. The accusation in the letter was serious, indeed—that Nehemiah intended to rebel, make himself king, and set up prophets. This report, says Sanballat, will be told to the king.

Possibly Sanballat wished to convey to Nehemiah that he wanted them to meet to see how they could put a stop to the rumor. More likely, however, Sanballat had learned that he could not fool Nehemiah, and he was reverting back to his scare tactics. The meaning would then be, "If you don't meet with me, I'll see to it that the king hears these things." This would seem to be confirmed by the fact that the letter he sent to Nehemiah was an *open letter*, (NRSV) that is, an *unsealed letter* (NIV). Such a letter could be read by anyone.

Perhaps Sanballat was telling the truth when he said *It is reported among the nations* that Nehemiah wanted to be the king of Judah, and that he had set up prophets *to proclaim such*. The prophets had taken on such a role before, both in the distant past (1 Kings 1:12-14; 11:29-31; 2 Kings 8:13; 9:1-3) and in the recent past (Haggai 2:20-23; Zechariah 3:6-7; 6:11). But Nehemiah was convinced that Sanballat was inventing the rumors to frighten them.

"They Are Coming to Kill You" (6:10-14)

Nehemiah's enemies changed their tactics once again. They hired Shemaiah to trick Nehemiah into going into the Temple to hide, on the pretense that some unidentified persons were coming to kill him. Nehemiah, however, discerned that Tobiah and Sanballat were behind the ploy, and he refused to go.

Verse 10 contains the only biblical reference to *Shemaiah the son of Delaiah*. Some have thought he was a false prophet—there was a false prophet by that name in Jeremiah's day (Jeremiah 29:31-32)—but it is more likely that Shemaiah was a priest. Laypersons were not allowed near the altar (Numbers 18:7), and neither he nor Nehemiah seemed to think it improper for Shemaiah to enter the Temple.

It is not clear why Nehemiah went into the house of Shemaiah. Apparently he had been summoned there. Nor is it clear why Shemaiah had been shut up. We are not even certain what is meant by the term *shut in*, (NIV) though it is usually assumed that Shemaiah was *confined* (NRSV) to his house for some reason. But if so, how could he leave his house to go to the house of God? Priests often lived in houses located within the courtyard of the Temple. If that were true of Shemaiah, it would explain how he could move from his house to the house of God so easily. It would also confirm our belief that Shemaiah was a priest.

Verses 11-13 give three reasons why Nehemiah refused to go into the Temple. First, *should a man like me runaway*? That is, it would not be proper for the governor to hide from danger. How could he then hold the respect of the people? Secondly, would a man like me *go into the temple to save his life*? Only priests were allowed in the Temple; laypersons entered at the threat of death (Numbers 18:7)

Nehemiah's third reason he shares with his readers, but not with Shemaiah. He understood that God had not sent him, but that Tobiah and Sanballat had hired him.

Nehemiah was not taken in by Shemaiah's pretense of concern. Shemaiah's real purpose was *that I should . . . sin. . . so they could give me an evil name, in order to taunt me.* They could jeer at the governor who fled for his life, and point a finger at the layman who entered the Temple.

There may have been a fourth reason why Nehemiah refused to go into the Temple. The probabilities are that Nehemiah was a eunuch (see the commentary on 2:6). If so, this, too, would keep Nehemiah out of the Temple, for eunuchs were not allowed near the altar (Leviticus 21:15-24; Deuteronomy 23:1).

The prophetess Noadiah (verse 14) is unknown except for this one reference. Noadiah is a masculine name in Ezra 8:33. And in the Septuagint, Noadiah is here called a prophet rather than a prophetess. That may simply mean, however, that the Septuagint translators assumed *prophetess* was an error, since prophetesses were rare, and since *Noadiah* was known to be a man's name.

One ancient manuscript reads, "who were giving me warning" rather than *who wanted to make me afraid.* (NRSV) or *were trying to intimidate me* (NIV) That reading would mean that Noadiah and the rest of the prophets wanted to help Nehemiah, not harm him.

Probably both here and in verse 12, the name of *Sanballat* has been inserted into the text. Nehemiah seems always to put the name Sanballat before that of Tobiah in his memoirs. The Chronicler or some later editor, seeing this story about Tobiah, and knowing that Sanballat and Tobiah were often linked in the memoirs, probably inserted the words *and Sanballat.* Also, the verb *had hired* (verse 12) is in the singular, indicating that only one person had hired Shemaiah. And here (verse 14), the words, *these things that they did* (NRSV) or *what they have done* (NIV) is a mistranslation. The Hebrew is in the singular: "these his works," referring to the deeds of a single person. Since we know that Tobiah had friends and in-laws in the city (see verses 17-19), it is reasonable to assume that he, rather than Sanballat, would be able to make contact with Shemaiah.

The Walls Are Completed (6:15-19)

Fifty-two days seems like a short time for the wall to have been finished. Josephus reports that it took two years and four months, and many are inclined to accept those figures as being more accurate. Four considerations, however, make fifty-two days not an impossible length of time. (1) Nehemiah organized the proceedings so that each person could work at full potential. (2) He instilled a sense of urgency in the people, and inspired them to work long hours and at great personal sacrifice. (3) The harassment of Sanballat and Tobiah made the people all the more determined to complete their task. (4) There were large portions of the wall that needed only minor repair.

All the nations surrounding Judah, according to the New Revised Standard Version and NIV, fell greatly in their own esteem. The nations recognized that they could not have accomplished this feat, and they stood in awe of Judah.

The Hebrew, however, is ambiguous at this point. What it says is, *Then they fell much in their eyes.* The question is, To whom does *they* refer? It could refer to the nations, and if so, the NRSV and NIV translation is correct. On the other hand, *they* could refer to *our enemies.* In that case, the meaning would be that Sanballat and Tobiah fell greatly in the eyes of the nations. For, in spite of everything these two could do, the Jews still were able to complete the wall. Either interpretation makes good sense, and it is impossible to tell which was meant.

The phrase *in those days* (verse 17) tells us that this account was written a good while after the events being described had transpired. It also suggests that these events happened repeatedly, over a long period of time. During that time, both Tobiah and his son married Jewish women of the city. These people naturally felt a loyalty to Tobiah. And others, perhaps because of business dealings, were bound by *oath* to him.

The name *Tobiah* (verse 19) means *goodness of the* LORD. How ironic that this man's name should have such a meaning! Nehemiah's words are sarcastic when he says the people spoke of the good deeds of *goodness of the* LORD. They also reported Nehemiah's words to him, apparently as a way of intimidating Nehemiah. Furthermore, he says, *Tobiah sent letters to intimidate me.* We are not told what threats were in the *letters*, but we cannot miss the point that Tobiah gave up neither easily nor quickly in his attempts to frighten Nehemiah.

The last part of chapter 6 would read more smoothly if verses 17-19 swapped places with verses 15-16. Verses 17-19 follow verse 13 more naturally than verses 15-16 do, and verses 15-16 make a better lead-in to chapter 7 than verses 17-19 do. There is no manuscript evidence, however, that any of these verses are out of sequence.

Leaders Appointed and People Counted (7:1-69)

The mention of *the singers and the Levites* in verse 1 is unexpected. These offices were associated with the Temple gates, not the city gates (see 2 Chronicles 23:19). Possibly a later copier or editor of the text added these words under the influence of Nehemiah 7:43-45; 10:28; Ezra 7:7, or some other place where the gatekeepers, the singers, and the Levites are mentioned together.

Two people are mentioned in verse 2—*Hanani and Hananiah.* Yet, the verse goes on to say *he feared God . . . .* Perhaps, then, *Hanani* and *Hananiah* are two forms of the same name.

In verse 3 Nehemiah is still taking precautions. If the gates were opened too early, the city would not yet be ready to defend itself in case of attack. The words, *each to his station,* show that Nehemiah was as methodical about stationing the guards as he had been about allotting sections of the wall to be repaired. Once again he assigns persons to work *beside his own house* (see 3:23). Perhaps Nehemiah felt a person would construct the wall more solidly and guard it more vigorously if the person were opposite his own house.

A walled-in area is not a city unless people live in it. Nehemiah's next task, therefore, was to populate Jerusalem. To see who was available, he found the book of the genealogy of those who came up at the first (verse 5).

The list that Nehemiah found (given in verses 6-69) is the same list that appears in Ezra 2 (but with several variations). The people are identified in Ezra 2:2 as those who came with Zerubbabel and Jeshua. These, of course, were not the first people to return to Jerusalem. But they were the ones who had built the Temple, and the Temple had been completed for seventy years before Nehemiah ever left Persia. For him, therefore, they were among those who came up at the first.

There is strong evidence that the list Nehemiah used is actually a combination of two or more lists. What we may have, therefore, is a list of those who returned with Sheshbazzar (see Ezra 1:8, 11), another list of those who returned with Zerubbabel, and perhaps a third list of those who returned after the time of Zerubbabel.

Some scholars believe the first part of Nehemiah's memoirs ends with 7:5, and that 7:6-73a was added later. Other scholars include verses 6-73a in the memoirs.

The People Settle in Their Towns (7:70-73a)

Here, as in Ezra 2, the list of returnees is followed by a giving of gold, silver, and costly garments. However, in Ezra 2, the people gave in order that the house of God might be built *on its site* (Ezra 2:68-69). That was the project dearest to Ezra's heart. Here, however, the people *gave to the work*. When Nehemiah used the term *the work*, he was referring to the building of the city wall. That was the project closest to *his* heart.

The second half of verse 73 does not conclude what is said in chapter 7, but rather introduces what is said in chapter 8. The paragraphing in the NRSV and NIV indicates that this is so.

§ § § § § § §

The Message of Nehemiah 6–7

§ Before Jesus sent out his disciples on their missionary journey, he called them together to invest them with certain powers and to give them final instructions (Matthew 10). Among the charges he gave to them was this one: *Be wise as serpents* (NRSV) or *shrewd as snakes* (NIV) *and innocent as doves* (Matthew 10:16). Nehemiah would have known exactly what Jesus meant. That was his strategy in dealing with Sanballat and Tobiah.

It is not always easy to be wise as serpents; sometimes it is even harder to be innocent as doves. But Nehemiah gives us a helpful model so that we might understand more clearly how to put Jesus' words into action.

§ It would have been easy for Nehemiah to have considered his job done once the walls were built. That, after all, was the task he was sent to Jerusalem to do. But though that was a great achievement, and one in which Nehemiah undoubtedly took great pride, he knew he could not stop there; there was still a job to do. Nehemiah heard God's call, after the wall was built, to repopulate the city. If we do not hear God challenging us to go a step further, is God not speaking, or are we not hearing?

§ § § § § § § §

Nehemiah 8–10

Introduction to These Chapters

Anyone reading through the book of Nehemiah for the first time will not be prepared for what comes in chapter 8. After seven chapters of Nehemiah's determination to finish the wall in spite of problems and difficulties, both external and internal, suddenly we are back to the story of Ezra. Nehemiah will not appear again until chapter 11. There are two exceptions—Nehemiah is mentioned in 8:9 and 10:1.

Here is an outline of these chapters.

I. The Reading of the Law (7:73b-8:12)
II. The Feast of Booths Observed (8:13-18)
III. A Day of Repentance (9:1-37)
  A. Confession and praise (9:1-5)
  B. Ezra's prayer (9:6-37)
IV. The Covenant Renewed (9:38-10:39)

The resumption of the Ezra story here in the book of Nehemiah has puzzled readers and fascinated commentators for centuries. The obvious question is, Why? Why does Ezra suddenly appear as the main character in a book that up to this point has not even mentioned him? Does this portion of the Ezra story belong here? Or did it get misplaced? If the latter, was it misplaced accidentally or on purpose? And if on purpose, we are back to the question, Why? What reason did the Chronicler (or some later editor) have for putting a portion of the Ezra story here?

Let us answer the first question first. Does this portion of the Ezra story belong here? The answer is almost certainly, No. If Nehemiah arrived in Jerusalem in 445 B.C., and Ezra in 397, then it would have been impossible for Ezra to have read the law of Moses to the people immediately following the fifty-two days it took to repair the wall. But even if we say that Ezra came to Jerusalem during the seventh year of Artaxerxes I, in 458, we are left with an unanswerable problem. Why would Ezra, who was sent to Jerusalem to teach the law to the people, wait thirteen years to do so? He is represented as coming to Jerusalem carrying the law of God in his hand (Ezra 7:25), and eager to get started teaching it (Ezra 7:10). It is unlike Ezra to put off the task closest to his heart. It seems best, then, to say that this portion of the Ezra story has been misplaced. It probably originally followed Ezra 8.

We can only guess about who put the story here, and why. Most probably, the Chronicler (or, perhaps, a later editor) placed the Ezra material here. Earlier, the Chronicler rearranged some material because it suited his purpose to do so (see Ezra 4:6-24). And once again his theological interests dictated that he place this story here. He wanted to show that the people who settled in the restored city had committed themselves to living by God's laws. The people are listed in chapter 7; they hear the word read in chapter 8; they repent in chapter 9; and they "set their seal" to the covenant in chapter 10. They are then ready to populate Jerusalem in chapter 11.

The Reading of the Law (7:73b–8:12)

The similarity between verses 7:73–8:1 and Ezra 3:1 is inescapable. The *seventh month* was Israel's most important month for religious festivals. It is no accident that it was this month that was chosen for this assembly.

The *Water Gate* was on the eastern wall, outside the Temple area. Some believe the assembly was held there so that all could attend, including women and children, and men who were ritually unclean. Others, however, believe that this square is the same as the *open square* referred to in Ezra 10:9 and the *square on the east* in 2 Chronicles 29:4. If that is so, then the assembly took place within the Temple complex.

The *book of the law of Moses* was that book of law which Ezra had brought with him from Persia. Although some scholars believe this was the book of Deuteronomy only, it probably was the entire Pentateuch.

It is not clear who is meant when the text says *they* told Ezra to bring the book. Grammatically, *they* would refer to all the people. However, that is an impossibility. Perhaps the leaders of the people are meant. It is obvious that the whole assembly was prearranged.

All who were able to understand (verse 2) probably refers to children old enough to understand. The question arises, however—if both men and women were there, plus all the older children, who was watching the infants and young children? Probably there were servants to do this (see 7:66-67).

According to verse 3, Ezra read for approximately six hours. During all that time all the people were attentive.

Verses 4 through 8 describe five aspects of the ceremony which correspond closely to the synagogue worship practices of a later day. It is possible that this description was influenced by later practice, but it is also possible that later practice continued the ritual described here. The synagogue arose while the people were in exile, and it is not unlikely that this ceremony reflects the pattern developed there. The elements that correspond to later practice are mentioned below.

The wooden pulpit (or, literally, tower) on which Ezra stood, was made *for the purpose* (NRSV) or *for the occasion* (NIV), that is, especially for this occasion. Perhaps so. But the word translated purpose or occasion means *word*, and is so translated in the Old Testament more than 300 times. This tower or pulpit, then, was made *for the word*, that is, for speeches. Perhaps, then, the tower was not new, but commonly used whenever a speaker addressed a large crowd. The tradition was continued in the synagogue that the speaker spoke from a raised platform.

Thirteen persons are named as having stood with Ezra. This was a way of emphasizing their support for what Ezra read. This practice was continued in the synagogue service, too, by having seats of honor near the raised pulpit for distinguished scholars (compare Matthew 23:2, 5-7).

It is strange that thirteen men stood with Ezra. Six on each side would have been symbolic (representing the twelve tribes of Israel), and seven on each side would have been symbolic (seven being the perfect number). But six on his right and seven on his left is unusual. The last name mentioned on Ezra's left is *Meshullum*. Some have wondered if this name were not originally the similar-looking Hebrew word meaning *on his left hand*.

When Ezra opened the book of the law (verse 5), all the people stood. The practice of standing for the reading of the Scriptures was a third practice continued in the synagogue; it passed from there into Christian worship.

Fourth, the lifting of one's hands, with palms up and eyes skyward, became a conventional posture for prayer in the synagogue (see verse 6). The practice of worshiping with faces to the ground is continued today by the Muslims.

Once again in verse 7, thirteen men are named as those who helped the people understand the law. These are not the same men, however. Only one name is repeated, that of Maaseiah, and since no lineage is given in either case, it is impossible to know whether the same man is meant.

What does it mean to say the thirteen men *gave the sense* (NRSV) of the reading (see verse 8)? It may mean simply that they *were giving the meaning* (NIV) of the laws to the people. It is possible, however, that so many of the people no longer understood the Hebrew language that as the laws were read in Hebrew, these men translated them into Aramaic so the people could understand what was being read (compare 13:23-24). If so, this is the fifth element in this service which corresponds to, or was continued in, synagogue practice. The later rabbis so interpreted this passage, and pointed back to this event as the beginning of the Targums.

Verse 9 is the first of two places where Nehemiah is mentioned in chapters 8–10. Most Old Testament scholars agree that the name of Nehemiah does not belong here. Three reasons are usually given. First, the mention of Nehemiah confuses what is otherwise a straightforward story about Ezra. Secondly, the verb *said* is in the singular (indicating that and the Levites who taught the people is also secondary). And third, it seems improbable that Ezra and Nehemiah were in Jerusalem at the same time, for several reasons. (a) For all the reasons mentioned earlier (Introduction to Ezra, pages 7-10; Introduction to Nehemiah, pages 54-56), it seems probable that Nehemiah came to Jerusalem in 445 B.C., and Ezra in 397. If their time in Jerusalem overlapped at all, Nehemiah must have been a very old man when it did. (b) The responsibilities assigned to Ezra and to Nehemiah by the king were so similar that it strains the imagination to say that the two men were to conduct their activities in the same place and at the same time. (c) It is strange that two men, assigned to work simultaneously with the same small group of people, would carry on their work quite independently of each another. (d) To say that Nehemiah was present when the events of Nehemiah 8 took place is to say that Ezra waited thirteen years to put his work into effect. And that, as we have seen, is uncharacteristic of Ezra.

The day was *sacred* (NIV) or *holy* (NRSV) *to the* LORD because it was the first day of Israel's holiest month (see 8:2). The people wept when they heard the words of the law, presumably out of contrition (compare the reaction

of King Josiah in 2 Chronicles 34:19, 21). They are told
not to weep because the law commanded that the people
rejoice (Deuteronomy 16:9-11 and 13-14, for example).

To *eat the fat* and *drink sweet wine* (NRSV) or as the
(NIV) translates *to enjoy choice food and sweet drinks,* (verse
10) was to indulge in the finest the land had to offer.
Portions, however, were to be sent to him for whom
nothing is prepared, that is, for the poor. Israel was never
to forget the poor.

The Feast or Festival of Booths Observed (8:13-18)

On the second day the leaders of the people came
together again to study the law with Ezra. It was on this
occasion that they discovered written in the law a
command that the people should dwell in booths during
the feast of the seventh month. This commandment is
found in Leviticus 23:42. Nowhere is it written in the law,
however, that they should proclaim in all their towns
that the people should bring branches to make booths.
Nor do the branches the people are told to gather
correspond exactly with those prescribed in the law (see
Leviticus 23:40). Probably the thought was that any leafy
trees would do.

According to verses 16-18, the people *celebrated the feast*
(NIV) or *festival* (NRSV) *seven days.* Ezra *read from the book
of the law* during the entire seven days, and the people
rejoiced. On the eighth day, however, there was a solemn
assembly, as the law commanded (Numbers 29:35).

The reference to *Jeshua* (NRSV) or *Joshua (NIV) the son
of Nun* (verse 17) should, perhaps, read *Jeshua the son of
Jozadak,* since such a celebration was held in the days of
Jeshua and Zerubbabel (Ezra 3:2). The other possibility is
that this was the first time since Jeshua the son of Nun
that the people had actually dwelt in booths when
observing this festival.

Many scholars believe that the Ezra story ends here, at
the close of Nehemiah 8. Ezra is mentioned in Nehemiah

9:6, but only in the Greek text, not in the Hebrew. Others believe all of Nehemiah 8–10 belongs to the Ezra story, and originally stood between Ezra 8 and Ezra 9.

A Day of Repentance (9:1-37)

Because of the abrupt change of mood between chapter 8 (rejoicing) and chapter 9 (penitence), many believe this chapter is out of place. Some would place it after Ezra 10, since that chapter deals with foreign wives, and this chapter repents for that sin. Others would leave this chapter in the book of Nehemiah, but put it after chapter 13, since that chapter, too, deals with the sin of marrying foreign women. Wherever the chapter was originally, the probabilities are that the Chronicler moved it to its present position to show that the people who populated Jerusalem repented of their sins before doing so.

Confession and Praise (9:1-5)

Fasting, sackcloth, and earth upon their heads are all signs of anguish, remorse, and mourning.

According to verse 2, the people not only confessed their sins, but the iniquities of their fathers as well.

They read from the book of the law for a fourth of the day (see verse 3). But who are *they*? Grammatically, *they* would refer to *the Israelites* of verse 2. Probably, however, the Levites of verse 4 are meant. The second *they* in the verse however, does refer to all the people.

Verse 4 is the only place the *stairs of the Levites* (NRSV) or *on the stairs where the Levites stood* (NIV) are mentioned. We cannot be certain what these stairs were. Probably they led to the platform from which Ezra had spoken earlier (8:4). Eight Levites are named.

Eight Levites are named again in verse 5. They are called *the Levites*, as if they were the official group of Levites for the occasion, yet only five of them are the same as those named in verse 4.

The call to bless the Lord *from everlasting to everlasting* is strange on two counts. First, one cannot be commanded to do something in the past. And second, only God exists from everlasting to everlasting. There are two possible solutions. One is to say that the meaning is simply, *Bless the* LORD *for evermore* (compare Psalm 115:18). More likely, however, is the second solution. Notice that the second half of the verse is addressed to God, *Blessed be your glorious name.* Perhaps that prayer really begins with the word *from.* The people are told to stand and bless the Lord; then begins the Levites' prayer, *From everlasting to everlasting blessed be thy glorious name.*

Ezra's Prayer (9:6-37)

The rest of chapter 9 is a long prayer, attributed to Ezra (9:6). The words *and Ezra said,* however, do not appear in the Hebrew text. The NRSV has taken these words from the Septuagint (Greek) version of the Hebrew Bible. Many commentators believe that originally this prayer had nothing to do with the story of either Ezra or Nehemiah. It was a typical Jewish prayer of that day (compare, for example, Psalms 78, 105, 106, 135, and 136). The Chronicler placed it here (if the interpretation given above is correct) as the continuation of the Levites' prayer begun in verse 5.

The prayer emphasizes both the greatness and the grace of God in dealing with the Israelite people. Throughout their history, the people had been unfaithful to God, but God had dealt with them in kindness (see 9:16-17 as typical). To be sure, God had to punish the people as a way of bringing them to repentance (9:26-27). But God's punishment was always for the purpose of redeeming the people, never for the purpose of reprisal.

The ending of the prayer is confusing unless we are willing to admit that it comes from a time later than either Nehemiah or Ezra. We are slaves this day, says verse 36. The rich yield of the land goes to the kings whom you have placed over us because of our sins . . . *and we are in great distress* (verse 37). That is contrary to the situation faced by Nehemiah or Ezra. They were not slaves; on the contrary, they had just returned from exile. Nor did either Nehemiah or Ezra feel malice toward the Persian kings. Rather, they believed the kings had acted in accordance with the will and purpose of God. (See Ezra 1:1-5; 4:3; 6:1-15; 7:6, 11-28; Nehemiah 2:5-8.) The situation described sounds much more like the fate the Jews suffered under later Greek rule (333–168 B.C.) than under the Persian kings. The Chronicler put this prayer here because it suited his purposes to do so. The people who will occupy the land in chapter 11 must first repent of their sins (chapter 9), and covenant to keep God's law (chapter 10).

The Covenant Renewed (9:38–10:39)

The Chronicler is now ready for the people to make a firm covenant and write it, and to have their princes, Levites, and priests set their seal to it.

In verses 1-26, those who set their seal, or, in modern terms, who signed the document, are listed. The absence of the name of Ezra is striking evidence that this story originally did not belong to the Ezra material.

We have already seen why the Chronicler placed this chapter here. But where did it go originally? One good possibility is that it stood after Nehemiah 13. To see why, compare 10:30 with 13:23-27; 10:31 with 13:15-22; 10:34 with 13:31; 10:35-37 with 13:31; and 10:37-39 with 13:12. Furthermore, it is reasonable to expect the people to covenant together not to do these things after Nehemiah had initiated the reform movement, rather than before. Most scholars, therefore, believe chapter 10 originally followed chapter 13. That would make chapter 10 the final chapter of Nehemiah's book. The last sentence of this chapter, then, would be not only an appropriate response to Nehemiah's question of 13:11, but also a fine ending to the book.

§ § § § § § §

The Message of Nehemiah 8–10

§ Ezra knew the importance of having interpreters available to help the people understand what the Scriptures said (Nehemiah 8:8). In the same way, interpreters can help us as we read the Scripture.

§ The people who came together to study God's laws with Ezra understood quite well that what the law commanded, they were to do (see Nehemiah 8:14-16). We need to understand the Bible in the same way.

§ The prayer attributed to Ezra (Nehemiah 9:6-37) points out the grace of God in dealing with the people. Although grace is primarily a New Testament word, the concept is as old as the first sinners who knew themselves forgiven of their sins. We, like the children of Israel, often refuse to obey. But God is ready to forgive, is slow to anger, and is abounding in steadfast love (9:16, 26). Of course, God will punish, if we continue to disobey, but the purpose of the divine punishment is always to bring us to repentance (9:29-30).

§ Some have felt the concerns of Nehemiah 10:30-39 to be of little consequence. They do not comprise "the weightier matters of the law" of which Jesus spoke (Matthew 23:23). But the situation Nehemiah faced was different. In Jesus' day the Pharisees had become masters of the details of the law; in Nehemiah's day, the people were neglecting these details altogther. Nehemiah was determined that they would *not neglect the house of our God* (10:39). We need to hear these words again today. For, though we frequently give lip service to the weightier matters, we often neglect doing even the simplest tasks for the house of God.

§ § § § § § §

EZRA, NEHEMIAH, AND ESTHER

Nehemiah 11–12

Introduction to These Chapters

Chapter 11 continues the story which was left hanging in chapter 7. Very quickly, however, the history is again interrupted by a series of lists (11:3–12:26), and when it resumes in 12:27, we are once again surprised. For here we read of the dedication of the wall, an event we might have expected to find much earlier.

Here is an outline of these chapters.

I. Nehemiah's Plan to Populate Jerusalem (11:1-2)
II. Those Living in Jerusalem and Judah (11:3-36)
III. Post-exilic Priests and Levites (12:1-26)
IV. The Dedication of the Wall (12:27-43)
V. According to the Command of David (12:44-47)

Nehemiah's Plan to Populate Jerusalem (11:1-2)

Although government and religious leaders lived in Jerusalem, not many of the common people did. Nehemiah, therefore, asked the rest of the people to *cast lots* to see who would move into the city. Apparently most were reluctant to move, for *the people blessed* (NRSV) or *commended* (NIV) those who offered to do so.

Notice the religious nature of Nehemiah's plan. The casting of *lots* was a way of discovering God's will. Those upon whom the lot fell, therefore, were divinely chosen to live in Jerusalem. Notice, too, that it was one out of ten who was chosen. Earlier we were told that the Levites received the tithes from the people, and that the priests received a *tenth of the tithes* (NIV) or *tithe of the tithes*

(NRSV) (10:38). Now a tithe of the people is selected to inhabit *the holy city*.

Those Living in Jerusalem and Judah (11:3-36)

In verses 3-24, the Chronicler lists those people who lived in Jerusalem. He begins with the lay leaders (verses 3-9), then lists the priests (verses 10-14), the Levites (verses 15-18), and the lesser officials (verses 19-24).

The list in verses 4-6 of those of the tribe of Judah is unexpectedly short. The similar list in 1 Chronicles 9 is longer.

Shilonite (NRSV) should read, *Shelanite*. The Shelanites were descendants of *Shelah* (NIV), a son of Judah, who was the father of the tribe of Judah (see Genesis 38:1-5).

The term *valiant warriors* (NSIV or *able men* (NIV) usually refers to military heroes, and sounds out of place here. For this reason, and for other reasons that will be discussed later, many Old Testament scholars believe the lists inserted here were originally military lists.

The Hebrew text in verse 8 is unintelligible. Various reconstructions have been suggested, but none is completely satisfactory.

No ancestry is given for *Jachin* (verse 10). Some believe the name of *Jachin* should be read as *the son of*, thus making the entire series of names in verses 10-11 the ancestry of one priest, *Jedaiah*. There is no textual support for such a translation, however, and the name of *Jachin* is found in the list of priests in 1 Chronicles 9:10.

The term *supervisor* (NIV) or *officer* (NRSV) *of the house of God* may be a synonym for high priest. Notice, for example, that the high priest Azariah is called *the chief officer of the house of God* NRSV or in the NIV in 2 Chronicles 31:13. The official in charge of the temple of God

Again we find a military phrase, *valient warriors or able men*, which seems out of place in a list of priests. The name *Haggedolim* means *the great ones*. This is the only occurrence of this name in the Bible, and seems strange as the name of an individual person, since it is the plural form. But if it is not a proper name, and should be translated literally, its reference is unclear. Possibly this is another military reference.

The phrase *the outside work of the house of God* (verse 16) has no specific reference. Perhaps it means the maintenance of the building. Or, it may refer to the collecting of the tithes. We cannot be sure.

Mattaniah was a descendant of *Asaph*, who had been appointed as one of the singers in David's day (1 Chronicles 15:16-17), and to whom several of the psalms are attributed (Psalms 50; 73–88).

Bakbukiah is mentioned only here and twice in Chapter 12. No genealogy is given for him in any of these places. It is impossible, therefore, to be certain of his lineage. One cannot help but notice, however, how similar his name is to the name of Bakbuk, whose descendants returned with Zerubbabel (Ezra 2:51). But the sons of Bakbuk were Temple servants (Ezra 2:43). So if *Bakbukiah* is a descendant of Bakbuk, his family has moved from being Temple servants to Levites, and *the second among his associates* at that!

Only two *gatekeepers* are mentioned in verse 19. First Chronicles 9:17 lists four, while Ezra 2:42 and Nehemiah 12:25 each name six.

Verse 20 leads us to believe the Chronicler is now turning his attention to the rest of Israel *in all the towns of Judah*. As a matter of fact, however, verses 21-24 continue to list those in Jerusalem. Not until verse 25 do we read of those *in all the towns of Judah*. Furthermore, the information found in verses 21-24 is missing in the parallel account in 1 Chronicles 9. This leads us to suspect that verses 21-24 were inserted into the text by a copyist or editor.

Ophel was the site of the city of David before it was expanded by later kings. The name *Ophel* means *swelling* or *protuberance*. It is the singular form of the word translated *tumors* in 1 Samuel 5:6 and other places.

Some believe David was the king referred to in verse 23. If so, however, we have no record of the command he gave concerning *a settled provision for the singers* (NRSV). The NIV translates it: *the singers were under thhe king's orders, which regulated their daily activity.* The reference may be to the Persian king, since Persian kings often took an interest in the religious practices of their subjects.

With verses 25-36, the lists of those living in Jerusalem are now completed, and the Chronicler turns his attention to those in *the villages.* First he lists *the people of Judah* (verses 25-30), then *the people of Benjamin* (NRSV) or *descendants of Benjamin* (NIV) (verses 31-36).

Some of the towns of Judah listed in verses 25 through 30 are a good deal farther from Jerusalem than we should expect the returned exiles to be living. For, to say the people *camped from Beersheba to the Valley of Hinnom* (NRSV) (verse 30) is to say that they were living all the way from Beersheba to the Valley of Hinnom (NIV) that is from one end of the territory of Judah to the other. That means some of the returnees were living in the territory ruled by Geshem the Arab. That is hardly what we would expect.

It is possible that this is a stylized list, more or less copied from Joshua 15 or some similar source. Another possibility is that it was originally a list of fortified cities. We have noted before the use of military language in these lists—valiant warriors and ablemen (verses 6 and 14) and now the word *camped* (NRSV) which the NIV translates as *living* (verse 30).

Furthermore, some of the towns listed here are known to have been military posts along the southern border of Judah in pre-exilic days. All this, plus what is yet to come in verses 31-36, suggests that what we have here are lists of available warriors and fortified cities which the

Chronicler or some later editor modified and used for his own purposes.

The Benjaminite towns are listed in verses 31-36. As in the case of the towns of Judah, some of the Benjaminite towns are farther from Jerusalem than we would have expected, and once again they represent border towns. Others were located on the main road leading to Jerusalem. These facts once again raise the question of whether these might not have been garrison cities intended to protect pre-exilic Judah's borders and capital city.

Post-exilic Priests and Levites (12:1-26)

When Zerubbabel and Jeshua returned to the land of their ancestors in 520 B.C., Jeshua became the first high priest of the post-exilic era. The priests and Levites who served with him are listed here—the priests in verses 1-7, and the Levites in verses 8-9. These lists are longer than the parallel lists in Ezra 2 and Nehemiah 7. One clue that some material has been added to what was originally written is the appearance of the word *and* before the name of *Joiarib* in verse 6 (omitted by the New Revised Standard Version and NIV). Presumably the Chronicler's list ended with *Shemaiah*, but some later editor who had additional information added the word *and*, and the six names following it. This speculation is strengthened if not confirmed by the fact that the same thing is true in verse 19. Once again the word *and* precedes the name of *Joiarib* (once again omitted by the NIV and NRSV).

Jeshua (verse 10) was the son of Jozadak (Ezra 3:2), the high priest who was taken into exile by Nebuchadnezzar (see 1 Chronicles 6:15). This list of high priests from *Jeshua* to *Jaddua*, therefore, continues the list in 1 Chronicles 6:3-15.

According to Josephus, *Jaddua* was high priest during the time of Alexander the Great. If this is accurate, Jaddua ruled during the third, and perhaps the fourth quarter of the fourth century B.C. (Alexander died in 323 B.C.) This is later than most scholars believe the Chronicler lived (though some date the Chronicler as late as 250 B.C.), and Jaddua may, therefore, represent a later insertion.

Joiada's son was not *Jonathan*, but Johanan, as he is called in verses 22 and 23. In Ezra 10:6, he is called *Jehohanan*, and he is called Jehohanan in extra-biblical sources as well. Apparently a copyist simply made an error as he copied verse 11.

In verses 12-21, the Chronicler now brings us back to *the days of Joiakim*, and lists the priests of that day. He gives a personal name for each of the family names given in verses 1-7, except that the names of Hattush and Rehum are omitted, the name of *Harim* added, and six of the names are spelled differently. None of the priests listed is known to us, with the exception of *Zechariah* of the house of Iddo (verse 16). The chances are good that this is the same Zechariah who was a prophet (see Zechariah 1:1 and Ezra 5:1).

We should expect a list of Levites to follow the list of priests. For that, however, we must wait until verses 24-26. Verses 22-23 contain a note, probably an insertion into the text, indicating that the names of the Levites and also the priests were recorded from the days of Eliashib to the time of Jaddua.

The Book of the Annals mentioned in verse 23 is not the same as our First and Second Chronicles, but rather was an official record to which this editor had access.

The Dedication of the Wall (12:27-43)

The Chronicler has taken us all the way to the day of Jaddua and Alexander the Great; now he jumps back to the dedication of the wall, which had been completed more than a century earlier. The logical place for this story would have been immediately following 6:15, at the completion of the wall. Possibly that is where the story stood in Nehemiah's memoirs. For, if 12:27-43 is placed between 6:15 and 6:16, the transitions at both ends of this story are very smooth. Many scholars believe, therefore, that that was where the story was put originally, and that it was lifted from there, and placed here.

But why would the Chronicler move this story? The answer is that it was very important to the Chronicler that those who dedicated the city wall were not themselves defiled. Just as the repopulating of Jerusalem had to wait until the people had heard the reading of the law, repented for their sins, and renewed the covenant, so also the people were not fit to dedicate the wall until these things had been done.

According to verse 27, the Levites had to be brought to Jerusalem, for although the leaders lived in Jerusalem (see 11:1), the Levites did not (see 11:20, 36).

The town of Netophath (verse 28) was just south of Bethlehem.

According to verse 30, the priests and Levites purified themselves, the people, the gates, and the wall. We are not told what rituals or disciplines were enacted by the priests as they performed these functions. It is possible they followed the practices in Exodus 19:14-15 and Numbers 19:18.

The actual dedication service is described in verses 31 through 43. Nehemiah *appointed two great companies* (NRSV) *assigned two large choirs* (NIV) of people which went in procession, one to the right on the wall, and the other to the left. They met and came to a halt at the Gate of the Guard. There they sang, offered great sacrifices, and rejoiced.

The statement that *Ezra the scribe* went before them (verse 36) is considered by most scholars as an insertion into the text. Ezra came to Jerusalem some forty-eight years later than Nehemiah did. They were not contemporaries. Even so, there may be justification for adding Ezra's name to this climactic event, for he deserves as much credit as Nehemiah for molding the post-exilic community into a cohesive religious body.

Apparently, the *Gate of the Guard* mentioned in verse 39 was not in the wall of the city (it is not mentioned in Nehemiah 3), but was an inside gate. The Hebrew word may mean *prison* or *guardhouse*, as well as *guard*. Nehemiah 3:25 speaks of *the court of the guard* (using the same Hebrew word) next to the upper house of the king. This implies that the guards were bodyguards rather than keepers of a prison. The passage draws a picture of a guardhouse next to the upper house of the king, with a courtyard (3:25) surrounded by a wall in which there was a gate (12:39).

Compare verse 43 with Ezra 3:13.

According to the Command of David (12:44-47)

The closing verses of chapter 12 and the opening verses of chapter 13 (verses 1-3) paint an idealistic picture of the restored community. From the days of Zerubbabel to the days of Nehemiah (verse 47), the people of Judah rejoiced over the priests and the Levites (verse 44). These priests and Levites performed their duties according to the command of David, as did the singers and the gatekeepers (verses 44-45). The people gave the *daily portions* and set aside certain portions for the Levites (verse 47). The Levites, in turn set aside portions for the priests (verse 47). According to these verses, then, things were as they should be up to the time of Nehemiah.

But this is an obvious exaggeration. If the system had worked that well, Nehemiah's reforms (in chapter 13) would not have been necessary. Why, then, would the Chronicler indicate that everything ran smoothly *in the days of Zerubbabel and in the days of Nehemiah* (verse 47)? The answer is, he wanted his readers to know that the oath taken by the people in 10:28-39 was genuine, and that the abuses of chapter 13 were not the rule, but the exception. Perhaps in doing this he overstated his case. But it was important for all to know that though some had *defiled . . . the covenant* (13:29), most had rejoiced in keeping the law.

§ § § § § § §

The Message of Nehemiah 11–12

There are several messages for us today in these chapters of Nehemiah.

§ When Nehemiah needed some people to populate Jerusalem, he asked the people to cast lots to see who would go. Some have criticized Nehemiah for this, saying he was shifting the blame from himself to God so the people would not get angry at him. But it could be that Nehemiah sincerely believed that those who lived in Jerusalem should be divinely chosen. In the same way, we today would benefit by seeking divine guidance before we make major decisions.

§ Sometimes it bothers us to hear that a later editor took what a biblical writer wrote, and altered it or moved it to a different place in the book. That sounds too much like tampering with God's word. However, these later editors were people of God, too. Their concern was that God's word come through loud and clear. Sometimes they felt they could enhance the hearing of God's word by moving one section of material to another place. God could work through these people as well as the original writers.

§ One of the most thrilling aspects of the dedication of the city wall is the note of joy and thanksgiving that comes through time and time again. Note verses 27, 31, 38, 40, and especially verse 43. No one could miss the note of *joy* in this verse. It is repeated like the refrain of a musical masterpiece. We, too, need to recapture the note of joy in our celebrations.

§ § § § § § §

Nehemiah 13

Introduction to These Chapters

The first three verses of this chapter belong with verses 44-47 of chapter 12. These verses continue the idealized picture of the Jewish cultic system with which chapter 12 concludes. Then we are told of the reforms Nehemiah put into effect. The chapter closes with a summary of Nehemiah's work and a prayer for God's favor.

Here is an outline of chapter 13.

I. Separation from Foreigners (13:1-3)
II. The Cleansing of the Temple (13:4-9)
III. The Restoration of the Levites (13:10-14)
IV. Enforcement of the Sabbath Laws (13:15-22)
V. Purification from Foreign Influence (13:23-29)
VI. Nehemiah's Accomplishments (13:30-31)

Separation from Foreigners (13:1-3)

On that day is a transitional phrase, and does not identify any particular day. This scene reminds us of the similar gathering recorded in Nehemiah 8. Perhaps the people came together regularly to hear the law read.

The place where it is recorded that Ammonites and Moabites should not enter the assembly of God is Deuteronomy 23:3. There, however, God's name, *Yahweh* (translated *the LORD*), is used. Nehemiah 13:1, in fact, is the only place in the Bible that speaks of *the assembly of God* rather than the assembly of Yahweh (the Lord). According to verse 2 it was both the Moabites, and the

Ammonites who hired Balaam. That story is found in Numbers 22–24 (where only the Moabites are mentioned). It is not strictly accurate to say that God *turned the curse into a blessing*, for no curse was ever uttered. What God did was to turn the intended curse into a blessing.

The law referred only to the Ammonites and Moabites; the people applied it to everyone of foreign descent. Furthermore, the law restricted the Ammonites and Moabites only from the official assemblies; the people required that they be *separated from Israel* (NRSV)—that is, banned—and *excluded* (NIV) from their presence.

The Cleansing of the Temple (13:4-9)

The words, now *before this* (verse 4) are supplied, perhaps by the Chronicler, but more likely by a later editor, since the Chronicler would have seen verses 1-3 as part of the idealized picture of 12:44-47. After this transitional phrase, we once again have first-person material, taken from Nehemiah's memoirs.

Eliashib the priest may not have been the same Eliashib who was high priest (3:1, 20; 13:28). We would not expect the high priest to be appointed over the chambers or storerooms of the house of our God. On the other hand, the high priest was the *supervisor or officer* (NRSV) *of the house of God* (11:11) or *the chief officer* (NRSV) or *official* (NIV) of the house of God (2 Chronicles 31:13). Perhaps this was Nehemiah's way of laying the blame squarely at the high priest's feet. He who was ruler of the entire house of God could certainly have controlled what went on in the chambers.

We are not told how Eliashib was connected with Tobiah. It may have been by marriage or it may have been related to Tobiah's friendship with Sanballat (see verse 28).

The room prepared for Tobiah (verse 5) was a large chamber where they had previously put all the offerings which were for the Levites, other Temple officials, and the priests. It is not clear whether the offerings stopped coming in before or after Tobiah occupied the chamber.

Nehemiah served as governor of Judah for twelve years (5:14). Then he went to the king (verse 6), that is, back to Persia. We are not told how long he stayed in Persia, but after a while he asked for permission to return to Jerusalem. It was while Nehemiah was away from Jerusalem that Eliashib permitted Tobiah to move into the chamber of the Temple.

According to verse 7, what Eliashib had done was evil because Tobiah was a non-Jew. His presence in the Temple, therefore, made the Temple unclean. There also may have been a touch of indignation on Nehemiah's part because Eliashib and Tobiah had defied his authority.

The word translated *greatly displeased* (NIV) or *very angry* (NRSV) in verse 8 means *furious* or *enraged*. In his anger, Nehemiah threw Tobiah's furniture out of the chamber.

Then Nehemiah ordered that the chambers be cleaned (see verse 9). Notice the plural. It was not just the chamber where Tobiah lived, but everywhere he might have touched that needed to be cleaned. After the Temple had been made ritually pure again, Nehemiah brought the vessels and the offerings back to the chamber.

The Restoration of the Levites (13:10-14)

The *also* in verse 10 makes it sound as if what follows is a brand-new discovery, separate from and unrelated to the incident just described. But the word *also* does not appear in the Hebrew text, and the probabilities are that the discovery that the portions of *the Levites had not been given to them* was a direct result of Nehemiah's restoring of the chamber of the Temple. The chambers served as storehouses for the tithes intended for the Levites. When Nehemiah brought back the vessels, the cereal offering, and the frankincense for the chamber (verse 9), he undoubtedly asked about the tithes of grain, wine, and oil for the Levites (verse 5). It was probably at that time that he learned that the portions of *the Levites had not been given to them.*

Levites were forbidden by law to own property (Numbers 18:20-24; Deuteronomy 18:1-2). It is unclear, then, what is meant by *they had gone back to their fields.* There are three possibilities: The Levites had illegally bought some fields; they had been hired out to work the fields of others; or they farmed the fields in those villages where Levites usually lived (Netophah, for example; see 1 Chronicles 9:14*a*, 16*b*).

According to verse 11 the house of God had been *forsaken* (NRSV) or *neglected* (NIV) in the sense that the normal activities of the cult could not be carried on without the Levites. Nehemiah *rebuked* (NIV) or *remonstrated with* (NRSV) *the officials* for letting this happen. Some of the best Hebrew texts do not include the words, *with the officials.* It is possible, therefore, that Nehemiah rebuked or remonstrated with all of Judah.

After the Levites were once again in their stations (verse 11), the people brought grain, wine, and oil into the storehouses.

Verse 13 states that Nehemiah chose a priest, a scribe, and a Levite as *treasurers over the storehouses* (NRSV) or *in charge of the storerooms* (NIV). Apparently Nehemiah believed in equal representation among the segments of Judean life. If Hanan was the grandson of Mattaniah of 12:8, then the singers also were represented among the treasurers.

In verse 14, Nehemiah closed his description of this reform with a prayer asking that God remember him, and not wipe out his good deeds. The Hebrew word carries the sense of faithfulness. Nehemiah had been more than just a man of good deeds; he had been faithful.

Enforcement of the Sabbath Laws (13:15-22)

Nehemiah was appalled by the lack of respect for the sabbath. Both Jews and foreigners were working on the sabbath, bringing in wares, and buying and selling goods in Jerusalem. Nehemiah warned them (or, witnessed to them—the Hebrew word carries both meanings) not to do that any more. To the *men of Tyre* (NIV) ir *Tyrians*) (NRSV), however, sabbath regulations had no significance. Their religion did not forbid working on the Jewish sabbath. Nehemiah *remonstrated with* (NRSV) or *rebuked* (NIV) *the nobles of Judah* (compare verse 11). It is not clear whether *the nobles* were engaging in this *wicked* (NIV) or *evil thing* (NRSV), or whether Nehemiah remonstrated with them for allowing the people to. Verse 18 implies that *desecrating* (NIV) or *profaning the sabbath* (NRSV) was the sin of their fathers that caused God to bring evil on them and on the city. There is support for this view in Jeremiah 17:21-27, but more typical of the prophets is a passage like Ezekiel 22:6-16, which sees a whole host of sins as the cause of the downfall of Jerusalem.

Verse 18 reminds us of Ezra 9:13-14. The argument in both places is, seeing how great a tragedy was brought upon us by the sins of our fathers, shall we make things worse by repeating those same sins?

Nehemiah, never one to rely upon moral persuasion alone, took steps to ensure that the sabbath laws would be kept (see verse 19). First, he ordered that the doors of the gates be shut before dark on the day before the sabbath, and that they not be opened until after the sabbath. He stationed some of his servants at the gates to make sure no one slipped by.

According to verse 20, Nehemiah's plan worked inside the city walls, but apparently it was business as usual just outside Jerusalem.

Nehemiah observed the flouting of his reform outside the city walls for a sabbath or two (verse 20), then he warned the people that if they continued to disobey he would *lay hands on* them. Nehemiah meant either that he, personally, would bring physical harm upon them, or that as governor of Judah, he would have the offenders arrested. Whatever the threat was, it worked. *From that time on they* did not come on the sabbath.

Why did Nehemiah have the Levites guard the gates (see verse 22)? That was not a regular part of their duty. Perhaps it was merely to give his own servants some relief (see verse 19). Probably, however, it was because Nehemiah saw this as a religious duty. The Levites were not just guarding the gates of the city; they were guarding the law of God *to keep the sabbath day holy*. For that reason, the Levites had to purify themselves before assuming guard duty.

Once again Nehemiah closed the description of his reform with a prayer for divine favor.

Purification from Foreign Influence (13:23-29)

The final issue Nehemiah dealt with was the issue of mixed marriages. This was an ever-recurring problem (see Ezra 9–10; Nehemiah 6:18; 10:30; 13:1-3). For the first time, however, marriages to women of Ashdod are mentioned.

Verse 24 is a difficult verse. First, it is not clear whether the Hebrew means the children spoke a garbled language, half in one language and half in another, or whether it means, as most modern translations interpret it, half the children *spoke the language of Ashdod, and* could not *speak the language of Judah*. Secondly, the Hebrew text speaks of "the Jewish language." There is no such language. Hebrew is undoubtedly meant, and the NRSV and NIV do well in translating it as *the language of Judah*. Third, the words, *the language of other peoples*, is a guess on the part of the translators. The Hebrew text is unintelligible at this point. The reason for Nehemiah's concern, however, is clear enough.

Once again in verse 25 Nehemiah's anger took control of his actions (compare verse 8). Did he merely speak harshly to the offenders when he cursed them, or did he actually lay a curse upon them? While either would be intimidating, the latter would carry the greater consequences. And why did he pull out their hair? Some have thought it was a way of forcing a show of grief on them (pulling out one's own hair was a way of expressing grief). In light of the fact that Nehemiah also beat the offenders, however, it seems more likely he pulled out their hair in a burst of anger rather than for any symbolic purpose.

The incident referred to in verses 26-27 is found in 1 Kings 11:1-11. The point Nehemiah is making is this: if Solomon, as great as he was, succumbed to idolatry because of his marriages to foreign women, do you think you would fare any better?

Nehemiah had fought with Sanballat all during the days he was rebuilding the wall. He had won that battle, and probably thought he was through with Sanballat. But here his old enemy crops up again. One of Sanballat's daughters had married the grandson of Eliashib the high priest. That was a triple offense. It was bad enough for any Jewish man to marry a foreign woman; it was doubly so for a man in the family of the high priest (Leviticus 21:14). But for him to marry the daughter of Sanballat was simply intolerable. Nehemiah undoubtedly counted that as a personal slap in the face. He therefore chased him away, and probably from Jerusalem as well.

Once again Nehemiah closed the description of his reform with a prayer (see verse 29). This time, however, the prayer was different. It did not ask for divine favor for himself, but for divine disfavor for Eliashib.

Nehemiah's Accomplishments (13:30-31)

Nehemiah summarized his accomplishments, all three of which have to do with Israel's worship: He cleansed Israel from everything foreign; he established the duties of the priests and the Levites, and he provided for the offerings, the festivals, and the tithes. He said nothing of his work in constructing the wall, for he was thinking only of his second term as governor.

For the fourth time in this one chapter, Nehemiah closed the description of his reform with a prayer (see verses 14, 22, and 29). That was entirely appropriate, for Nehemiah had done everything for the Temple and for God (verse 14).

§ § § § § § §

The Message of Nehemiah 13

Chapter 13 gives us an example to follow, a question to ponder, and a warning to remember.

§ Many of us become righteously indignant when we see someone being mistreated, but few of us do anything about it. It is easy to diagnose the problem and point an accusing finger. It is easy to feel sympathy for the one wronged. But after all that has been done, the wrong still remains. Nehemiah did not just bewail the offense; he took action calculated to put an end to it, and to reestablish the right. We may not approve of all of Nehemiah's methods, but at least he reminds us that more is required of us than words and sympathetic feelings. Nehemiah has given us an example to follow.

§ Some express dismay over Nehemiah's religious intolerance. Should not our religion be open-minded and generous-spirited? Should we not respect and welcome every human attempt to find God's will? Shall we consider every human understanding of God equally valid? Can we mix our Christian concept of God with another, and still have what God has revealed to us through Jesus Christ? Will a tolerant religion result in a watered-down religion? That is at least a question to ponder.

§ The forces of evil once defeated are not forever destroyed. If Nehemiah did not know that before he returned to Jerusalem, he surely learned it while there. His two terms as governor of Judah were full of defeated enemies rising up again, and battles won having to be refought. What was true in Nehemiah's day is true today. A nation once reformed cannot be assumed to stay that way. Nor can the church. Nor can our personal lives.

§ § § § § § §

Introduction to Esther

The book of Esther is intensely interesting and masterfully told. Esther must have been especially interesting to the Jews in exile during Persian rule. For, in the midst of the humiliation known only to a conquered people scattered throughout an alien empire, here is the story of a Jewish woman who became queen of that empire. And it is the story of a crafty Jewish man who turned the tables on the second most powerful person in the kingdom, and eventually took that man's place as second in command. It is the story of the "divine reversal" of fortunes, God protecting the chosen people and bringing to ruin those who sought to harm them.

The book of Esther has been much beloved by Jews over the centuries. Scores of hand-copied texts have survived from the Middle Ages, more than any other book in the Old Testament. Medieval Jewish scholars produced more commentaries on Esther than on any other book in the Hebrew Bible except the books of Moses (Genesis through Deuteronomy). It was often said Esther ranked second in importance only to the Torah because it was the book that kept the Jews alive. It was a clarion call to fight back against enemy aggression. The Jews had been inspired by this call, not just during the days of the Persian Empire, but throughout the centuries. Some said Esther was even more important than the Torah, for Judaism could exist without the Torah, but it would have been exterminated without the book of Esther.

But this book, beloved though it is, has also been an

embarrassment to sensitive Jews and Christians. Nowhere in its ten chapters is God ever mentioned. Nor are prayer, worship, or any of the great religious festivals mentioned. The great themes of the Old Testament are lacking—themes like the Exodus from Egypt, the receiving of the Ten Commandments, and the making of the covenant. Even the great virtues taught in the rest of the Bible are missing. Instead, we have a story in which vengeance plays a primary role.

The secular nature of the book and the ethics it espouses have been matters of concern from the beginning. Even at the council of Jamnia in A.D. 90, when Esther was officially adopted as part of the Hebrew Bible, some rabbis objected. And some Christians resisted its inclusion in the Christian Bible until the Council of Carthage in A.D. 397. Luther, at the time of the Protestant Reformation, said he wished Esther had never been written, and not a few Christians today raise the question of why such a book is included in the Bible. Yet it is not entirely fair to characterize the book as secular.

God Plays an Important Role

We spoke earlier of the "divine reversal" of the fortunes of the characters in the story of Esther. The story is full of coincidences, quirks of fate, and little ironies that make for delightful reading. But when it is read on a different level, the book is a powerful statement about God's activity and the working out of the divine will even in those situations when God is silent, and seems to be nowhere about. The fact that God is not mentioned in the story does not mean God was not active in the proceedings.

Additions to the Text

The book of Esther comes to us in three editions, one in Hebrew and two in Greek. The Hebrew version is the shortest and the earliest. But it was one of the Greek versions, the so-called "B text," that found its way from the Septuagint to the Vulgate, and from there into use by Christians until the time of the Reformation. Today, Roman Catholics and the Orthodox Churches still use the longer version of the story, while Protestants use the shorter version, and consider the Additions to Esther as part of the Apocrypha.

History or Short Story?

The book of Esther has been interpreted in three ways. Some think of it as a record of historical events that took place while the Jews were in exile and Ahasuerus was king. Whereas this is certainly possible, none of the events in the book can be verified by non-biblical sources, and many of them contradict what we know from our knowledge of history. Ahasuerus is the only character in the story whose historical reality is certain, and there is some disagreement even there as to which king is meant.

Most Old Testament scholars hold to a second possibility, namely that the Book of Esther was written not as history, but as a short story, or a historical novel.

The third possibility is to regard Esther as a mythical story describing the conflict between the gods of Babylon and the gods of Elam. Esther could represent the Babylonian goddess Ishtar, and Mordecai the Babylonian god Marduk. Similarly, Haman and his wife, Zeresh, could represent the Elamite god Humman and his wife Seres, while Vashti, the deposed queen, could represent Mashti, the Elamite goddess.

Theoretically, any of the above interpretations of Esther is possible. A large majority of Old Testament scholars, however, favor the second interpretation. Esther is a short story, written to amuse, to instill a sense of pride into a defeated people, and to assure in an ever-so-subtle way that God does not leave the course of history in the hands of those who rely only upon the sword.

Introduction to These Chapters

In the longer, Greek version of the story of Esther, used by the Roman and Eastern sectors of the church, the book begins with a dream in which God's plans are revealed to Mordecai. In the version of Esther that appears in the Protestant Bible, the story begins with a banquet given by Ahasuerus, King of Persia. The story moves on to show why Queen Vashti was deposed, and how Esther was chosen as Vashti's replacement. Finally, we learn of Mordecai's good deed toward the king, and the fact that Mordecai's deed was recorded in the king's chronicles.

Here is an outline of these chapters.

   I. King Ahasuerus Gives Three Banquets (1:1-9)
  II. Queen Vashti Is Deposed (1:10-22)
 III. Esther Is Selected as the New Queen (2:1-18)
 IV. Mordecai Notifies the King of Danger (2:19-23)

King Ahasuerus Gives Three Banquets (1:1-9)

Who was *Ahasuerus*? The Persian records make no mention of a king by that name. The Septuagint called the king Artaxerxes, based, apparently, upon some similarities in the lives of Ahasuerus in the Book of Esther and Artaxerxes II in Persian history. The identifying words, who reigned *from India to Ethiopia*, (NRSV) or *Cush* (NIV) however, would rule out Artaxerxes II, and limit the search to those kings between

Darius I (522–486 B.C.), who added northwest India to the empire, and Darius II (423–404), who lost Egypt. Not until the last quarter of the nineteenth century was evidence found that gave a positive identification of Ahasuerus. Inscriptions were uncovered in which the name of Xerxes I was given in three languages, and from these it became clear that Ahasuerus was Xerxes I (486–465).

The number of Persian satrapies varied from twenty to thirty-one. These were divided into *provinces* (compare Daniel 6:1).

Susa (verse 2) was one of four locations the Persian kings used as capital cities, the other three being Babylon, Ecbatana, and Persepolis.

The first banquet, described in verses 3-4, is for all the officials in the kingdom. *A hundred and eighty days* is an incredible length of time for a banquet to last. Many have tried to soften it by saying this allowed for all the nobles and governors of the provinces to come on a rotating basis. Even so, the question must be asked, Who was running the government during those six months?

Notice that this banquet plays no part in the story that follows.

According to verse 5, the king gave a second banquet for the men in Susa. This banquet lasted seven days.

At least a part of the purpose of these banquets seems to have been to enable the king to show off his riches and splendor (verse 4). Verses 3 and 4 give a vivid impression of the king's wealth.

Golden goblets have been unearthed by archaeological digs around Susa.

Persian law, according to Josephus, was that when the king drank, all the guests drank. That, however, is contradicted by the words, *each guest was allowed to drink in his own way* (NIV). Perhaps the meaning is, *no one was restrained* (NRSV). That is, each could drink all he wanted. The other possibility is that no one was forced to drink more than he desired.

According to verse 9, the third banquet, the *banquet for the women*, was given by Queen Vashti. Perhaps it would be more accurate to say that Vashti served as hostess for the banquet, for the author emphasizes that the banquet was held in the palace which belonged to King Ahasuerus.

Queen Vashti Is Deposed (1:10-22)

Apparently the king, when *merry with wine* (NRSV) or *in high spirits from wine* (NIV), if not routinely, thought of the queen as an object to be displayed even as were his riches (the word *display* (NIV) or *show* (NRSV) in verse 11 is the same word that is used in the past tense in verse 4). The Targums interpreted verse 11 to mean that Vashti was to appear before the men wearing only her royal crown. That, however, is not stated. But whatever it was that Vashti was told to do, she considered it to be an indignity, and she refused to do it.

The king was enraged (NRSV) or *became furious* (NIV). Not only had he been disobeyed; he had been embarrassed in front of all his men (verse 5). And his anger burned within him.

Nothing more is said of the banquets. Apparently they were disbanded after that incident. Later, the king inquired of his wise men what the law said should be done in such a case.

There are several things here that are not expected. First, why did Ahasuerus consult these wise men? Was he not capable of deciding on his own what to do? Secondly, the term *wise men* (NIV) or *sages* (NRSV) is usually associated with astrologers, and the words *who knew the times* (NIV) or *laws* (NRSV) sound as if astrologers are meant. Yet, they are described as versed in law. Third, Ahasuerus asked them what was to be done *according to the law*, yet the answer he received was based more on practical wisdom, as one might expect from an astrologer, than on the law.

Earlier (verse 10) we read of the seven eunuchs who served Ahasuerus. Here (verse 14) we are told of *the seven nobles* (NIV) or *officials* (NRSV) who had *access to the king . . .* that is, who were trusted enough to have personal contact with him daily. In Ezra 7:14, we read of the seven counselors of Artaxerxes. It was not just in Judaism that *seven* was considered a number that signified good.

Here (verse 19), in 8:8, and in Daniel 6:8, 12, 15, we read that the laws of the Persians and the Medes cannot be altered. There are no extra-biblical sources for that law.

It seems ludicrous that the king would send letters to every province indicating that *every man* be master or ruler in his own house (see verses 21-22). Does the king's wounded pride go even that far to seek revenge?

The words *and speak according to the language of his people* have generally been interpreted as meaning that the husband should not speak the language of his wife, if it were different from his own.

Esther Is Selected as the New Queen (2:1-18)

How long after *these things* does the author mean? The banquets were held in the third year of the king (1:3); the new queen was selected in his seventh year (2:16). It took a year to prepare the young women to see the king (2:12). That leaves three years unaccounted for. In Persian history, Xerxes was fighting the Greeks for two of those years.

Apparently Ahasuerus remembered Vashti with affection, since his anger cooled. Perhaps he even realized how childishly he had acted.

In verses 2-4, we see that once again the king seems helpless to devise a plan of his own.

Herodotus said that the Persian kings had to marry nobility. Specifically, the queen had to be selected from one of seven families. Certainly the procedure followed here goes against that custom.

Mordecai not only was a Jew; he was a descendant of *Kish*, the father of Saul (1 Samuel 9:1-2). The importance of this relationship will become apparent in the next chapter.

Who had been carried away from Jerusalem by Nebuchadnezzar? Certainly Mordecai cannot be meant, for that would make him some 120 years old at the least. Yet if Kish is meant, then this must be a Kish other than Saul's father, though he could be of the same family.

Hadassah (verse 7), which means *myrtle*, was Esther's Jewish name. *Esther* may come from the Persian word meaning *star* or it may come from the name of the Babylonian goddess, Ishtar.

Adoption was not provided for in the Mosaic law. It was practiced by other ancient civilizations, and apparently taken over by the Jews during the Exile. Adoption becomes a key theological concept in the New Testament.

In verse 9, we are not told why Hegai was so pleased with Esther. Perhaps he knew the king's tastes, and surmised that Esther would be chosen. Or perhaps he was personally attracted to her, and favored her for that reason. The third possibility is that the statement that Esther *won his favor* implies an active role, perhaps even a wily pursuit, on her part.

We are not told what Esther's *portion of food* (NRSV) or *special food* (NIV) consisted of, but we may be sure it did not conform to the Jewish dietary laws. Unlike Daniel, who found himself in a similar situation, Esther did not refuse the king's food (compare Daniel 1:5, 8). The Additions to Esther make the claim that the foods did not violate the Jewish laws.

Notice again the use of the number seven. Hegai provided Esther with seven chosen maids.

It is difficult to see how Esther could have kept secret her people or kindred with Mordecai present every day in front of the court of the harem in order to keep an eye on her. For, Mordecai's Jewishness was well known (see 3:4).

The "rules of the game" are laid out in verses 12-14. It is not clear, however, whether the things given to each maiden when she went in to the king were hers to keep, or whether they were simply provided for her use, and were to be left in the palace.

The *another part of the harem* (NIV) or *second harem*, (NRSV) apparently, was for the king's concubines as distinguished from his wives.

Again, Esther followed the advice of Hegai (see verse 15). If the women were allowed to keep what they took with them, it may be that Hegai's advice was that she take very little so as to not give the impression that she was trying to enrich herself at the king's expense.

It is not clear who is meant by all *who saw her*. They could be the other maidens in waiting, or they could be the seven chosen maids (verse 9). Also, the phrase could refer to others to whom Hegai showed her beauty (compare 1:11).

In verses 16-17, we are not told how many virgins preceded Esther (see the commentary on 2:1), but *the king loved Esther* (NRSV) or *was attracted to Esther* (NIV) *more than all* the others. If she were not the last, the others did not get their chance, for Ahasuerus *set the royal crown on her head*.

According to verse 18, the king gave another great banquet. Also, he granted *a holiday to the provinces*. At least, that is what the New Revised Standard Version and NIV say. The Hebrew says Ahasuerus "caused a rest" in the provinces. That could be interpreted as the granting of a holiday. Others have interpreted the words to mean that Ahasuerus granted freedom to prisoners or release from military service. Out of these possibilities, it seems most likely that he granted a holiday. Ahasuerus *gave a great banquet* to all his officials and nobles, and declared a holiday so that all could rejoice in the selection of a new queen.

We are not told who were the recipients of the *gifts*

that Ahasuerus gave freely, nor do we know exactly what these persons received.

Mordecai Notifies the King of Danger (2:19-23)

The story now shifts back to Mordecai. Esther has found favor with the king; now Mordecai gives the king reason to favor him.

Verse 19 says that Mordecai was sitting at the king's gate. Perhaps he had nothing else to do (compare 2:11), or he was wealthy, and therefore free of work obligations. Or, perhaps he was doing a part of his job. That is, he may have been a government official of some kind. The story does not tell us (but see the commentary on 3:2).

In verse 20, Esther's obedience to Mordecai is stressed once again (see verse 10). Technically, she never disobeyed Ahasuerus, yet she was able to get anything she wanted from him. Was her obedience to Mordecai of the same kind? (Compare also the commentary on verse 9).

We are not told the nature of Bigthan's and Teresh's complaint against the king. One of the Targums indicates it had to do with his selection of Esther as queen. *The doorway* (NIV) *threshold* (NRSV), also mentioned in 2 Kings 25:18 and Jeremiah 52:24, probably refers to the threshold or doorway of the king's quarters. If so, Bigthan and Teresh would have been two of the king's most trusted guards.

The Hebrew text indicates that Bigthan and Teresh were "hanged on the wood," or "on the tree." The NRSV and NIV probably correctly interpret this as *hanged on the gallows*. Some scholars, however, believe impalement was meant (compare Ezra 6:11), while others think crucifixion was. The same word is used in 5:14, however, and it is almost certain that "gallows" is the proper meaning there.

No mention is made of a possible reward for Mordecai. Rather, the deed was simply *recorded in the Book of the Annals*. It is perhaps not too strong a statement to say that kings never delayed such rewards. In this case, however, the plot of the story demands it.

The Message of Esther 1–2

§ Chapter 1 is replete with the signs of royalty and the opulence that goes with it. Twenty-one of the twenty-two verses in chapter 1 contain one or more of thirteen words which denote royalty (king, queen, kingdom, royal, reign, majesty, crown, palace, throne, and princes). The twenty-one verses use these words a total of fifty-seven times. The one verse that does not contain such a word (verse 6) describes the opulence of the king's palace, and notes the royal colors of the furnishings (white, blue, and purple). The splendor and unquestioned authority of the king seem to be evident everywhere. Yet throughout the story that follows, the king is portrayed as one who is sometimes disobeyed, who cannot make decisions on his own, and who is easily manipulated by those around him. What will it profit them, asked Jesus, if they gain the whole world and forfeits their life? (Matthew 16:26 and parallels).

§ Vashti was a brave woman. It took courage to refuse the king's command. She knew she would pay severely for her disobedience. Yet there were principles that stood higher with her than her good standing with the king. She would not degrade herself and all women by letting herself become an object to be gawked at.

§ It was undoubtedly intended as a compliment when it was said of Esther that she found favor in the eyes of all who saw her (2:15). Yet, how did she accomplish this? By keeping her heritage and her religion a secret, by ignoring Jewish customs, Jewish food laws, and Jewish worship practices. Jesus' question is again relevant: What will it profit a woman if she gains the whole world and forfeits her life?

§ § § § § § §

Introduction to These Chapters

The villain in the story is introduced in chapter 3, and immediately a conflict develops. That conflict leads to the decision to annihilate all the Jews in the kingdom. This in turn leads to a series of communications between Mordecai and Esther, and a decision on what must be done to stop the slaughter.

Here is an outline of these chapters.

I. Haman's Plot Against the Jews (3:1-15)
   A. Haman's Promotion, Mordecai's Defiance (3:1-4)
   B. Haman's Retaliation (3:5-15)
II. Esther Sees the King (4:1-17)

Haman's Promotion, Mordecai's Defiance (3:1-4)

Once again the chapter begins with the words *after these things* (NRSV) or *events* (NIV) (see 2:1). Once again, however, a considerable amount of time seems to have elapsed between chapters (see the commentary on 2:1). For, we are now in the *twelfth year of King Ahasuerus* (verse 7).

Haman enters the story with no introduction other than his genealogy (contrast the introduction of Mordecai in 2:5). His genealogy gives us enough information, however, for us to know that he and Mordecai will be enemies. Mordecai is a descendant of Kish, the father of Saul (2:5; 1 Samuel 9:1-2), and Haman is a descendant of Agag, Saul's bitter enemy. This, at least, is the common understanding of this verse. Some scholars hold that the term *Agagite* is Persian in origin, and has nothing to do with Agag, king of the Amalekites during the time of Saul. As far back as the time of Josephus, however, the verse has been seen as setting the stage for inevitable conflict between Haman and Mordecai.

No reason is given for the promotion of Haman, just as no reason was given in chapter 2 for Mordecai's not receiving a reward (2:23).

Verse 2 could be interpreted to mean that Mordecai was one of the king's servants. Many commentators think so. The point is left vague by the author, since it is not critical to the story.

Why did Mordecai refuse to kneel down and pay honor to Haman? The only hint comes in verse 4—he was a Jew. But why would being a Jew make a difference? Jews frequently bowed to kings (1 Samuel 24:8; 2 Samuel 14:4; 1 Kings 1:16). The Additions to Esther say it was because Mordecai would not bow down to anyone except God; the Targums report it was because Haman had an idol embroidered on his robe, so that to bow before him was also to bow before a pagan idol. Neither of these explanations is verified in the (Protestant) Scriptures, however, and both seem to be attempts to supply a religious motive for Mordecai's action. If Mordecai were aware of Haman's ancestry, that in itself would have been motive enough.

According to verses 3-4, *the king's servants* (NRSV) or *royal officials* (NIV) were not willing to let the matter drop. Why should Mordecai be allowed to get away with disobeying the king's command? They therefore told Haman of Mordecai's defiance.

Haman's Retaliation (3:5-15)

Haman assumed that if Mordecai's refusal to bow before him was based on Mordecai's Jewishness, all Jews might be expected to do the same. The solution, therefore, was to destroy all the Jews in the kingdom.

If verse 7 were extracted from the story, the first-time reader would never suspect that anything was missing. It is not necessary to the story, and the transition from verse 6 to verse 8 is very smooth. The purpose of the verse is to select the date on which the pogrom would be held. The date selected was the thirteenth day of *the twelfth month*, though the day has been lost from this verse (see verse 13). It is not clear who *they* are ("he" in the Hebrew), though probably a "wise man" is meant.

Verses 8-9 make the point that Haman must now secure the permission of Ahasuerus to carry out his plan. He did not name the offending group, but simply told the king that they do not obey the king's laws. Then he offered his solution to the problem. It never seemed to dawn on the king that Haman had a personal axe to grind, even though Haman offered the king *ten thousand talents of silver* for the privilege of carrying out his plan.

Again proving how easy it was to manipulate him, Ahasuerus gave his blessing to the plan without even asking who the offending people were (see verses 10-11).

The *signet ring* was used to make the king's identifying mark. This mark guaranteed the authenticity of the document. For the king to give Haman his signet ring, therefore, was to give him authorization to do whatever he pleased. Not only that, the king did not even accept Haman's money. The money is given to you, he told Haman, and the people also (but see the commentary on 4:5-7).

According to verse 12, the people were told eleven months in advance that the slaughter was coming. Perhaps this advance notice was to cause more grief for the Jews by making them anticipate the horrors. Or it may have been a literary device to allow Mordecai and Esther time to devise a way to counter the attack.

The notice of the coming slaughter was sent on *the*

thirteenth day of the first month (verse 12), the day before the Passover observances were to be held (see Exodus 12:1-11). That detail heightens the suspense, since the Passover celebrated the deliverance of the Jews from the Egyptians. The question would be raised in the mind of every Jewish reader of the book, Will God deliver us once again?

Why did the couriers go quickly (verse 15)? The decree was issued eleven months in advance! The answer is that the Persians took great pride in their postal system. It was used only for the king's business, and the couriers sought to please the king by delivering each message as rapidly as possible. Indeed, it is doubtful that the couriers were even aware of the contents of the decree they carried.

There are four possible interpretations of the last sentence of this verse. (1) Least probable is the suggestion that the king and Haman sat down to drink in order to dull the remorse they felt for having issued such a decree. (2) Herodotus indicated that Persian kings always drank to a decision made while sober, and reconsidered when sober any decision made while drinking. Perhaps the king was simply following this custom. (3) A third interpretation is that the king and Haman, having finished the business at hand, had a friendly drink together. (4) Finally, there is the literary explanation. The people of Susa were *bewildered* (NIV)—"horrified" (NRSV) is probably the better word—at the royal decree. In stark contrast, *the king and Haman sat down to drink.* What better way to point out the lack of moral concern on the part of these two men?

Esther Sees the King (4:1-17)

Tearing one's clothes, putting on sackcloth and ashes, and wailing loudly were all signs of grief and distress. They were also signs of repentance, however, and some commentators think Mordecai was repenting for having caused the slaughter which was to come. More likely, he was wailing in distress. The fact that he went out into the city to do so indicates that he did not intend for his grieving to be private and personal; he was seeking support for his cause.

We are not told why one *clothed with sackcloth* was not allowed to enter the king's gate. It may have had something to do with a belief or superstition about death, since sackcloth was worn when mourning the dead.

Fasting was considered a religious activity by Jews, and was usually accompanied by prayer. Even though religion is not mentioned in this book, this is one of those signs that religion was not forgotten.

The Jews *lay in sackcloth and ashes*, that is, made their beds with such, only when their grief was extreme.

Some have thought this verse should follow 3:15. It would fit the sense there, and would not be missed here. Nevertheless, the thought is appropriate here as well.

Esther led a sheltered life as queen, and learned of Mordecai's mourning only through her *maids and her eunuchs*. She was very upset, and sent clothes to Mordecai so he could come inside the gate. Mordecai would not accept the clothes, however, for his time of mourning was not over.

According to verses 5-7, since Mordecai could not come inside the gate, Esther sent Hathach to Mordecai to see what was going on. Mordecai told Hathach everything that had happened, including *the exact sum* (NRSV) or *amount* (NIV) *of money that Haman had promised to pay* Ahasuerus for the privilege of annihilating the Jews.

How did Mordecai know how much money Haman had promised to give Ahasuerus? That, after all, had been said to Ahasuerus in a private conversation (3:8-9). But for security reasons the king was never left completely alone with anyone other than one of his wives or concubines. His attendants undoubtedly would have overheard the conversation with Haman, and we may assume that it was difficult then, as now, to keep government secrets confined to the palace.

Verse 7 offers no hint that Ahasuerus had refused Haman's offer to enrich the king's coffers. Indeed, the verse reads as if the plan were still in effect. Because of that, and because refusing the money seems so unlike what a king would do, many people believe that the original story did not include verse 3:11, at least not in its present form. (See the commentary on 7:4.)

That Mordecai was in possession of a copy of the decree (verse 8) from Haman is another indication that Mordecai either was a government official of some sort, or had contacts who kept him informed. The Additions to Esther insert a copy of the decree after 3:13.

Esther was afraid to approach the king without being called first, because anyone who did this was killed unless the king held out his golden scepter. Normally, perhaps, she would not have feared approaching Ahasuerus. But since she had not been called for thirty days, she was unsure of her standing with the king.

It is not clear why Esther could not have requested a hearing with the king. That would not have placed her in any danger. Perhaps she feared she would be refused. But that is hardly likely, for in the end she chose the more dangerous way. Perhaps the reason is only because the story demands it. Details such as this give the story its drama and suspense.

Who are *they* in verse 12? (NIV translated "*they*" as *Esther's words*) Hathach had been an intermediary between Esther and Mordecai. Had he now been joined by others?

Mordecai's reply to Esther in verse 13 is both a challenge to action and a gem of common sense. If you think you will get into trouble by going to the king, consider what will happen to you if you don't!

What did Mordecai mean when he said *relief and deliverance* will arise from somewhere else (see verse 14)?

What other *quarter* (NRSV) or *place* (NIV) did he have in mind? It seems clear that he meant from God. Yet it would be wrong to contrast deliverance from God with the deliverance that would come through the help of Esther. For, that, too, would be deliverance from God. The meaning, then, must be that if Esther refused the opportunity to bring about relief and deliverance for the Jews, that would not keep the deliverance from coming. It would simply mean that God would have to use a different agent, another quarter, to accomplish the divine will.

Mordecai's next words—Who knows but that *you have come to royal position* or *Dignnity* (NRSV) *For such a time as this?*—are so obviously a reference to the providence of God that commentators have asked throughout the centuries why this author was so reluctant to mention God. We simply accept the fact that nowhere in the entire book are God, religion, or religious activities called by name.

The one truth about herself that Mordecai had insisted that Esther hide (2:10, 20) was now what he said must be revealed. Only if the king realized that his own queen was a Jew would he call off the intended massacre of the Jews.

Esther was convinced by Mordecai's arguments. Before she was willing to go to the king, however, she insisted on a three-day fast, for herself, her maids, and all the Jews to be found in Susa. Such a fast makes sense only if interpreted as a religious act. The Additions to Esther so interpret the fast, and also add prayers rendered by both Mordecai and Esther. As always, however, the Hebrew text makes no mention of religious motives or activities.

Esther's words, *if I perish, I perish*, are the words of one who has determined to do what she must, regardless of the consequences to herself. They should not be viewed, as some have suggested, as a statement of resignation. Nor should her decision to go to the king be thought of as the path of least harm to herself. Esther was unaware of what the consequences for herself would be. The chapter thus ends with suspense still high.

§ § § § § § §

The Message of Esther 3–4

These chapters speak to us of the cost of integrity, the importance of good leaders, the necessity of action, and the choice of reward.

§ Mordecai refused to bow to Haman. He knew the risk he was taking in defying the king's orders, but some things are more important than personal safety. Personal integrity is one of them.

§ If an elected official does not act according to our wishes, we can replace that person at the next election. The people in the Persian Empire were not so fortunate; they had no way to replace their king. Ahasuerus was a weak king, but all the more dangerous because of it. For, he was easily manipulated by the unscrupulous Haman. How important it is to have the right leaders!

§ The story of Esther could have had a very different ending. What if Mordecai had wailed in the streets of Susa, but nothing more? What if he had not devised a plan of action and convinced Esther to approach the king? The pogrom would have taken place. There are times to mourn and times to go into action. Fortunately, Mordecai knew when to end one and to begin the other.

§ From our earliest days we have been taught, "Honesty is the best policy." What we have to learn on our own is that honesty can be risky. Esther was fully aware of the risks when she told Ahasuerus the truth about herself. Things turned out well for Esther, but that is no guarantee they always will. Honesty is indeed the best policy. but in terms of earthly reward, dishonesty may pay the higher dividends. Where does our interest lie—in material gain that soon fades away or in spiritual gain that fulfills eternity?

§ § § § § § §

EZRA, NEHEMIAH, AND ESTHER

Esther 5–6

Introduction to These Chapters

Chapter 5 continues the narrative of chapter 4 and sets the stage for chapter 6, one of the most delightful parts of the story. Here is an outline of these chapters.

    I. Esther's First Banquet (5:1-8)
   II. Haman's Plot Against Mordecai (5:9-14)
 III. Mordecai Is Honored (6:1-14)
       A. The king decides to honor Mordecai (6:1-6a)
       B. Haman describes the perfect honor (6:6b-9)
       C. Haman is humiliated (6:10-14)

Esther's First Banquet (5:1-8)

The fast was to have lasted for three days, both night and day (4:16). Yet it was *on the third day* that Esther approached the king. *Put on her royal robes* is literally *put on royalty*. According to the Old Latin Versions, she also "beautified herself with ointment."

The author displays a thorough knowledge of the architecture of the king's palace. By standing *in the inner court of the* king's palace, Esther had already placed herself in jeopardy (see 4:11).

The Additions to Esther make this scene much more dramatic. Esther approached the king "frozen with fear." Ahasuerus looked at her in fierce anger, and Esther "turned pale . . . and collapsed." Then "God changed the spirit of the king to gentleness." Ahasuerus "sprang from his throne and . . . comforted her," promising that she would "not die." None of this drama, however, is in the Hebrew text.

The words *won his favor* (NRSV) or *he was pleased with* (NIV) are the same as in 2:15 and 2:17. Her beauty had put her in good stead then, and the implication may be that five years had not diminished her charm (compare 3:7 with *2:16*).

Archaeological digs at Susa have uncovered a relief in which the king sat on his throne holding a scepter.

To the half of my kingdom is typical oriental exaggeration. It was not intended to be taken literally. Oriental custom demanded that the first offer of generosity be refused. Only if the person making the offer insisted was the one being offered the gift to accept it. Both king and queen understood that. Ahasuerus knew Esther would not accept his offer, and Esther knew better than to try.

Why did Esther delay in making her request? Did she think the timing was not right, or that the king would be in a better mood after a banquet meal? Probably not. It is more likely that Esther was using the same oriental courtesies as the king. One's real request was never voiced in the first petition. It was only as the one granting the favor insisted on knowing the true request that the petitioner was free to voice it.

Esther told the king that the dinner had already been prepared. That means the sumptuous meal was prepared while Esther and all her maids were fasting (verse 16).

Why did Esther want Haman at the banquet? There are two literary reasons for it. First, the higher Haman has risen in honor, the greater will be his fall when it comes. Secondly, there is the striking contrast that the Jews are fasting because of the intended slaughter, while the one responsible for the pogrom is feasting. But Esther may have had a far different motive. Possibly she feigned an interest in Haman in order to turn the king against him.

The initial letters of the words, *let the king* and Haman

come this day, when written in Hebrew, are YHWH, which is the Hebrew word for "Yahweh," the divine name. Some ancient copyists, noticing this, called attention to it by writing these initial letters larger than the other letters. The original writer of the story probably did not intentionally arrange the words this way in order to make this one mention of God in the story. It was just a literary coincidence.

The king did not know what he was saying when he said *that we may do as Esther desires* (NRSV) or *asks* (NIV). He was thinking of the banquet, but that was not her real desire.

While they were drinking wine, that is, after the meal, the king reiterated his willingness to do whatever Esther asked. Why did Esther again delay her request? A literary explanation is, it heightens the suspense of the story. A psychological explanation might be, she lost her nerve. But possibly there was a tactical reason. It is just possible that Esther has here out-maneuvered the king. Her invitation was for the king and Haman to come to another banquet if it should please the king to grant her request. By accepting the invitation, therefore, the king obligated himself to do whatever Esther would ask of him.

The scene shifts. Not until the end of chapter 6 will the banquet be mentioned again. Now attention is focused on the rivalry between Haman and Mordecai.

Haman's gladness of heart turned quickly to anger at the sight of Mordecai, who continued to insult Haman by refusing to rise when he approached.

Haman had been quick to suggest what the king should do on an earlier occasion (3:8-9). And he will give the king advice in the future (6:7-9). But he was helpless in knowing what to do to solve his own problem. So he turned to his friends and his wife for advice.

Haman's wealth must have been great (see 3:9). To have many sons was considered a mark of distinction.

According to this story, Haman had ten sons (9:10). Jewish tradition said he had 208 sons in addition to these.

Haman did not suspect what Esther was planning or the connection between her and Mordecai.

Haman was so angered by Mordecai's contempt for him that he could not enjoy any of the blessings he had.

Zeresh's ready solution to her husband's problem reminds us of Jezebel's quick and cold-blooded solution to her husband's problem (see 1 Kings 21:1-14). As in 2:23, the New Revised Standard Version and NIV assume, probably correctly, that *suspended upon* means *hanged on it*, and that *the tree* or *the wood* means *gallows*. Some scholars, however, believe impalement is meant. The great height of the wood (fifty cubits is about seventy-five feet) cannot be used to substantiate either interpretation, for in either case, that is plainly higher than necessary. The wood is to be fifty cubits high in order to publicly humiliate and to make an example of Mordecai.

Tell the king to have Mordecai hanged, said Zeresh. She may have known the king's inability to make decisions, or perhaps she simply forgot for the moment that one does not order the king to do anything.

The advice of his friends and his wife pleased Haman, so, in spite of the fact that he had not yet checked with the king on the matter, he had the gallows built.

The King Decides to Honor Mordecai (6:1-6a)

As chapter 6 begins, we are aware of Haman's plan to get permission from the king to hang Mordecai before the two of them go to Esther's banquet. There will be no way, then, for Esther to intervene. She is not even aware of the plot. Then unfolds an incredible series of coincidences (or providential happenings).

(1) The king could not sleep that night. Why *that* particular night?

(2) The king decided to pass the time by having *the book of Chronicles; the record of his reign* (NIV) or *the book of records, the Annals* (NRSV) read to him. Why then? Why that book?

(3) The servants read that portion of the book which recorded how Mordecai had saved the king. Why that particular portion of such a large book?

(4) The king had never bestowed an *honor or distinction* (NRSV) or *recognition* NIV on Mordecai for this deed. Why not? And why had he not thought of that before?

(5) Haman arrived at the palace early, and had just gone into the outer court when the king asked for someone to help him decide on Mordecai's reward. What incredible timing!

(6) Neither the king nor Haman knew that the other wanted to talk about Mordecai—the king to honor him, and Haman to hang him on the gallows.

(7) Haman assumed it was he, himself, whom the king wished to honor.

Had any one of these seven circumstances not been true, the story could not have taken the turn it did.

The king could not sleep is literally, *the king's sleep had fled* (compare Daniel 6:18)

The book of records, the Annals (NRSV) was the same as *the book of Chronicles* (NIV) (2:23), or simply *the chronicles*.

Notice the variation in the spelling of Bigthana's name (compare 2:21).

It was unheard of for a Persian king not to reward his benefactors immediately (see the commentary on 2:23).

Neither Haman nor the king had slept that night. Haman stopped in the outer court because he could not enter the inner court without being summoned (see 4:11).

The king spoke before Haman had a chance to tell him why he had come to the palace so early. Many have called Haman vain because he assumed he was the one the king wanted to honor. And doubtless he was. But he had reason for such an assumption. He had been promoted to second in the kingdom (3:1); he was the only one who was invited to dine with Esther and Ahasuerus, and not just once, but twice (5:4, 8, 12). No one, he thought, stood in better stead with the king.

The word *delights* (NIV) or *wishes* (NRSV) denotes a

strong urge. The same Hebrew word is used in 2:14 to describe the king's desire for one of his concubines.

Haman Describes the Perfect Honor (6:6*b*-9)

Haman said (NRSV) or *thought* (NIV) *to himself* is literally, ". . . . said in his heart." The ancient rabbis used this verse as proof of the inspiration of the Book of Esther. How could the author know what Haman said in his heart, they asked, unless the author were inspired?

It has often been remarked that Haman's words would make a perfect aside in a play.

Since Haman believed he was the one to be so honored, he named those things that would bring the greatest honor to himself. It is not enough that the honoree should wear royal robes; they should be *robes . . . which the king has worn*. Likewise, the horse which the honoree shall ride should be one *the king has ridden*. Persian art has verified the practice of adorning the king's horse with a crown-like head ornament.

In his excitement, Haman forgot his court manners. He did not begin with the expected words of deference, "If it please the king" (see the commentary on 5:4). Ahasuerus, however, did not seem to notice.

Haman used incorrect grammar, due also, perhaps, to his excitement. He began with the words, *For the man whom the king delights* (NIV) or *wishes* (NRSV) *to honor*, but he never finished that thought. Instead, he began a new, but related, idea, *let royal robes be brought*, and so on. This is sometimes done by speakers and writers for effect (technically called an *anacoluthon*), but is more frequently done by persons who have not completely thought through what they want to say. In Haman's case, it was certainly the latter. His exhilaration at the thought of being honored caused him to make a false start with his description.

Haman Is Humiliated (6:10-14)

Verse 10 marks the turning point in Haman's fortunes. Until now everything had gone his way. True, he had been irritated by Mordecai the Jew, but he was about to get that score settled, or so he thought. And he was about to receive the highest honor yet bestowed upon him. But then, irony of ironies, he had to bestow upon the despised Mordecai the very honor he had so gleefully constructed for himself.

The question is often raised how Ahasuerus could honor one Jew while at the same time planning to annihilate all Jews. The answer is, Ahasuerus was unaware of the identity of those who were to be slaughtered. Haman never told him (3:8-9), and the decree that went out concerning them had been written by Haman (3:12). As incredible as it sounds, Ahasuerus had agreed to the assassination of a whole group of people without ever asking who they were.

Mordecai did not seem impressed with all the ceremonies. He returned to the king's gate, perhaps awaiting his chance to taunt Haman again. Haman, on the other hand, hurried home, thoroughly humiliated. The head was covered during times of extreme grief, and particularly when mourning the dead (see 2 Samuel 15:30). Perhaps Haman felt that his life was ruined, that he might as well be dead. Or, on a literary level, this action is intended as a portent of what is to come (see 7:8).

How ironic that after having given him such poor advice (5:14), Haman's friends should now be called *his wise men*. His wise men and his wife now believed Haman could not win in his battle with Mordecai. The reason they gave is that Mordecai is of the Jewish people. But they were aware of Mordecai's Jewishness before (see 6:13, where Haman tells Zeresh and his friends about Mordecai.

That the king's eunuchs brought Haman to the banquet does not imply that Haman in his grief had forgotten the banquet. It was standard oriental procedure for the king's servants to escort those invited to a royal banquet. To go *in haste* was to recognize the importance of both the king (compare 1 Samuel 21:8) and the king's guest. The king was not aware that Haman had been devastated by the ceremonies for Mordecai.

§ § § § § § §

The Message of Esther 5–6

§ Jesus once counseled his disciples to "be wise as serpents and innocent as doves" (Matthew 10:16). Esther was following that procedure in these chapters. She matched her wits against those of the king, and she won. Yet, all the while she acted in proper deference to the king. There is a lesson here for those who find themselves having to deal with an authoritarian person who acts on whims.

§ Haman had every reason to be happy—every reason except one. He had riches; he had many sons; he was second in command in the kingdom; he had twice been invited to dine with the king and queen—yet, still, there was Mordecai. He was so obsessed with his hatred for Mordecai that "all this does me no good." In the same way, we sometimes let one disappointment blind us to all the reasons we have to be thankful.

§ Paul gave the Romans good advice when he warned against thinking of ourselves more highly than we should (Romans 12:3). Had Haman followed that simple principle, and not assumed that he was the one the king wanted to honor, he would have saved himself much embarrassment.

§ § § § § § §

Esther 7

Introduction to This Chapter

The downfall of Haman, begun in 6:10, comes to its climax in 7:10. Verses 1-2 of chapter 8 perhaps should be included in chapter 7. Though the action centers around Haman, the emergent hero is Mordecai, and the movement of the plot is plainly in the direction of Mordecai's elevation to second in command. Here is an outline of these chapters.

   I. Haman Is Accused (7:1-6)
  II. Haman Pleads for His Life (7:7-8)
 III. A Third Accusation Against Haman (7:9-10)

Haman Is Accused (7:1-6)

At this banquet, as at the first one, it was after the meal, and while they were drinking wine, that the king asked Esther what her request was. Again he assured her of his intentions to grant whatever she asked.

Esther did not know of Mordecai's reward, of Haman's plot to kill Mordecai, or of Haman's humiliation in having to honor Mordecai. The king was not aware that Esther was a Jew, that Haman had made plans to hang Mordecai, or that Haman had been humiliated by honoring Mordecai. Haman did not know that Esther had any connection with Mordecai or with the Jews. But the time had come for the secrets to be unveiled, and it was Esther who had to begin the process.

Grant me my life—this is my petition. And spare my people—this is my request (NIV) or *Let my life be given me—that is my petition—and the lives of my people—that is my request* (NRSV). At this point, neither the king nor Haman could have been sure just what Esther meant. Only here did Esther address the king with the informal *your*. She was making her appeal on the basis of their relationship.

In verse 4, Esther explained why her life and the lives of her people were in danger. We are sold, she said, to be destroyed, to be slain, and to be annihilated. One can imagine Haman's eyes widening and his jaw dropping as he heard these words, for they were his words (see 3:13); he could not mistake them. The king, however, did not make the connection; he had to ask Esther who was planning to do this (verse 5).

What loss to the king did Esther mean? She must have been referring to the ten thousand talents of silver offered him by Haman (3:9). The impression is left by 3:11 that the king did not accept the money from Haman. As indicated in the commentary on 4:7, however, there are several reasons to believe he did.

(1) Refusing such a large sum of money does not sound like something a king would do. We cannot be sure what ten thousand talents of silver would be worth today, but it has been estimated at fifty million dollars.

(2) When Mordecai was in mourning, and sent a message to Esther by way of Hathach, he told Esther the exact amount of money that Haman had promised to pay into the king's treasuries for the destruction of the Jews (see 4:7). Nothing was said about the king's having refused it. Indeed, Mordecai's plea would lose much of its force if the king had refused the money, for Mordecai was implying that the king was paid handsomely to do this. If the king had refused the money, we would have to say either that Mordecai was unaware of that refusal (which seems unlikely in light of the fact that he was privy to the rest of the king's conversation with Haman), or that he was purposely deceiving Esther.

(3) Esther says, "For we are sold, to be destroyed . . . and to be annihilated." What does she mean, we are sold, if Ahasuerus had not accepted the money?

(4) If Ahasuerus had refused the money, what loss to the king did Esther mean? She was not, as some have suggested, speaking of loss of taxes. For then she would be saying that their becoming slaves would result in a loss of taxes, but their being annihilated would not. It is difficult to follow the logic of that statement.

If we assume that Ahasuerus kept the money, these four difficulties are resolved. Moreover, that would also explain why Esther was so reluctant to do what Mordecai said she must, for she would be asking the king to give up fifty million dollars. I would have held my peace, she said, if we had been sold merely as slaves. For, what is our slavery compared to ten thousand talents of silver for the king? But we are talking about our very lives!

Against all these reasons for saying Ahasuerus accepted the money, there stands only one reason to say he did not. That one reason is that in 3:11 Ahasuerus told Haman, "the money is given to you." But notice that the text nowhere says Ahasuerus did not accept the money; it simply says he offered to let Haman keep it. If we remember the oriental custom described in the commentary on 5:3, it becomes clear that this was simply an offer which the king never intended to be taken literally. Haman, well versed in such amenities, understood full well that the king had no intention of not accepting it. And here, in 7:4, Esther knew it would cost the king the equivalent of fifty million dollars in silver to keep the slaughter from taking place.

According to the words of verse 5, the king makes no connection between Esther's words and Haman's edict. Strictly speaking, the answer to the king's questions is not Haman, but Ahasuerus. Haman had not "sold" the Jews; he had bought the privilege of having them slaughtered. It was Ahasuerus who had "sold" them.

Would *presume* (NRSV) or *dare* (NIV) is literally *would fill his heart*.

Esther's danger was twofold. Not only was she asking the king to give up a huge sum of money; she was also accusing the second most powerful person in the kingdom. It was by no means certain that the king would choose Esther's charm over Haman's political acumen (or whatever ability he had that caused the king to make him second in command in the kingdom). Haman, however, seemed to have no doubts about whom the king would choose. He cowered *terrified before the king and the queen*.

Haman Pleads for His Life (7:7-8)

Several possibilities exist as to why the king left the room. (1) Perhaps his anger was so intense that he needed to cool off before deciding what to do. (2) Or perhaps he was now helpless to make a decision, since he had always depended upon Haman for advice (see 3:8-11; 5:14). (3) Or, Ahasuerus may not have been able to look at Haman, whom he now hated. (4) Perhaps he did not wish to condemn Haman, whom he still counted as a friend. (5) He could have needed some time to think. All these suggestions are possible. Perhaps the real explanation, however, is literary—the king had to leave the room in order to set up the scene for what follows.

It is frequently said that Esther was still reclining on the couch in the manner of one dining at a banquet. That, however, does not seem likely. It is difficult to imagine Esther in a reclining position as she nervously accused Haman in verses 3-6. It might well be, however, that Esther, as well as Haman, could sense that evil was determined against Haman by the king, and that in her confidence, she once again reclined on the couch.

Once again the storyteller is the master of irony. Haman had planned to have Mordecai the Jew hanged for not bowing before him; now Haman throws himself at the feet of Esther the Jew, begging for his own life.

The word translated *on* could mean *beside* or *against* as well as *on*.

Haman's fate seems to have been sealed, not so much by Esther's words as by the king's indignation at Haman's supposed assault on the queen in the king's presence and in his own house.

We are not told who *they* are. Presumably they were the king's eunuchs (see verse 9). These attendants of the king sensed just as surely as Haman and Esther did that the king had determined evil against Haman. The Romans and the Greeks had a custom—and presumably the Persians as well—of covering the head of one who had been sentenced to death.

Esther knew that Haman had not tried to rape her. Why did she not say so? Because she knew that if Haman lived, thousands of Jews would die.

A Third Accusation Against Haman (7:9-10)

Several questions are raised by Harbona's words. First, the king's attendants were expected to remain quiet, and certainly were not to enter into the conversation or the affairs of the king. Why, then, did Harbona speak? It may be that Harbona simply blurted out the news about the gallows in the excitement of the moment.

This piece of information had to be revealed in order that the irony of the story could come about (in verse 10). Neither the king nor the queen knew about the gallows; the information had to come from someone else. Harbona was the king's messenger—literally.

But secondly, why did Ahasuerus not reprimand Harbona for his impertinence? Probably because the king, too, was excited. He was glad to get the information. He seized upon it, and probably never gave a thought to the fact that it came from one of his eunuchs.

Third, how did Harbona know about the gallows? The story does not tell us. Probably he was one of the ones who had gone to Haman's house to bring him to the banquet (6:14), and had inquired about the gallows when he saw them. This was the explanation Josephus gave.

A new charge against Haman, in addition to the charge brought by Esther (verses 4-6) and the charge brought by Ahasuerus (verse 8). The charge here is that Haman planned to hang the very man who had saved the king.

The greatest irony of the story is that Haman was hanged on the very gallows he had built for Mordecai.

It was only after Haman had been hanged that *the anger of the king abated* (NRSV) or *the king's fury subsided* (NIV) (compare 2:1).

§ § § § § § §

The Message of Esther 7

§ How much is a human life worth? Ahasuerus had been given fifty million dollars to annihilate all the Jews. What would we do if offered such a sum in exchange for a few thousand lives? Are people worth that much?

§ Time is money. Time is also convenience. If Ahasuerus gave up ten thousand talents of silver to save a people, what should we be willing to give up?

§ In the commentary it was suggested that Harbona told the king about the gallows because of his excitement at the drama unfolding before him. There is another possible explanation, however. Perhaps Harbona was calculating rather than excited. In other words, he was an opportunist. As he saw the inevitability of Haman's downfall, he wished to contribute his additional knowledge about Haman in the hope of receiving a reward from the king. How should we act in similar situations?

§ The message of Esther 7 is a series of questions. How we answer these questions depends upon what we see as important—people, money, convenience, opportunity. Where do we as Christians stand? See Matthew 6:33.

§ § § § § § §

Esther 8–10

Introduction to These Chapters

Except for one detail, chapter 7 would have made a
fine closing for the book of Esther. Mordecai was
victorious in his battle with Haman, and Esther was
triumphant in her bout with possible death. One element
of the story remains, however—the scheduled slaughter
of the Jews is still on the royal calendar. Chapter 8 is
concerned with resolving that one detail.

Chapters 9 and 10 include what many scholars believe
to be a series of additions to the book. Chapter 9 is
necessary to the story if it is true that the purpose of the
book was to explain the origin of the festival of Purim.
Chapter 10 glories in the greatness attained by Mordecai.

Here is an outline of these chapters.

   I. A Second Royal Edict (8:1-17)
  II. The Slaughter of the Enemies (9:1-15)
 III. The Celebration of Purim (9:16-32)
 IV. The Greatness of Mordecai (10:1-3)

A Second Royal Edict (8:1-17)

The first two verses in chapter 8 belong with chapter 7.
They complete the reversal that takes place there.

The question is often raised as to how Ahasuerus could
give the house of Haman to Esther, since the house
belonged to Haman. There are two possible answers.
First, both Josephus and Herodotus tell us that according
to Persian law, all the belongings of one who had

betrayed the king became a part of the king's estate. The other possibility is that Haman's house already belonged to the king, and was used as a place of residence for his grand vizier.

Mordecai was now able to come *before* (NRSV) or *in the presence of the king* (see the commentary on 1:14) because Esther had explained his relationship to her—he was her cousin, guardian (2:7), and counselor (2:10, 20; 4:7-14).

We are not told when the king took the signet ring from Haman.

According to verses 3-6, in spite of the turn of events in chapter 7, and in spite of the honors bestowed on Esther and Mordecai in 8:1-2, the slaughter of the Jews was still scheduled to take place. Esther, therefore, fell at the feet of the king weeping. She pleaded for him to put an end to the evil plan of Haman the Agagite, which he had devised against the Jews. This is the first time we have seen Esther's compassion. We have witnessed her fear (4:11-12), her scheming (5:1, especially if we accept the Old Latin addition, *and beautified herself with ointment*; compare 2 Kings 9:30), and her cunning (see the commentary on 5:7-8). Now we see her tears.

Raising the golden scepter seems to mean that Esther was free to rise and speak to the king while standing. There is no hint that her life was in danger.

Esther had always approached the king in deference (5:4, 8; 7:3), but here she did so more than ever. Verse 5 contains four conditional clauses. The first and third emphasize Ahasuerus' position as king; the second and fourth emphasize Esther's charm and the king's fondness for her. Only after making both points twice did Esther repeat her request of 7:3. She wisely referred to the document, not as the king's edict, but as the letters devised by Haman.

Most scholars believe it was an exaggeration to say that the Jews were in all the provinces of the king. We are not certain, however, and though such a wide dispersion of the Jews seems unlikely, it is not impossible.

Again playing to the king's fondness for her, Esther bases her appeal on her own emotions. *How can I bear to see* the disaster that is coming to my people?

Some interpret verse 7 as indicating a special fondness for the Jews on the part of the king. Others understand the king to be saying, "I have done all I can do; the rest is up to you." In either case, the king gave Esther and Mordecai the authority to do what they deemed necessary to prevent the calamity (verse 8).

The reason for Haman's death is here given as because he would lay hands on the Jews. That is hardly the impression one gets from reading chapter 7.

The edict and the sending of the king's couriers (see verses 8:9-14) is patterned after 3:12-15. The edict went out two months and ten days after the first one (see 3:12 and 8:9). The Greek text indicates the edict went out on the twenty-third day of Nisan, rather than Sivan. Some prefer this reading, since that would mean no time was wasted in getting the edict out (only ten days having passed). Others, however, believe that the seventy days between the thirteenth of the first month (3:12) and the twenty-third day of the third month may have been intended as symbolic of the seventy years of exile.

The second edict contained details not found in the first one—the *hundred and twenty-seven provinces*, for example, were not mentioned in chapter 3 (compare 1:1); the writing to the Jews in their language was new; and the fact that the horses were bred from the royal herd was not mentioned earlier. What the *edict* allowed was also different, not to *annihilate* an innocent people, but to *defend* themselves.

Many have cringed at verse 11, for it seems to suggest that the Jews are to slaughter not only the attacking soldiers, but also their children and women. If the comma is removed after *them*, however, the sentence yields a different meaning—the Jews are to slaughter the soldiers who are attacking the Jewish children and women. This seems to be the preferable interpretation, since we should hardly expect the attacking soldiers to have their children and women with them.

Verse 15 describes Mordecai's appearance. He had not been dressed so regally since the day he had been honored by Haman (see 6:11). All the inhabitants of the city of Susa shouted and rejoiced at the appearance of Mordecai. Contrast the mood of the city of Susa after Haman's decree (see 3:15).

Those who *professed to be Jews* (verse 17) were either genuine converts, or they were pretenders, feigning conversion because of the danger they perceived. How that issue is decided depends in part on where we believe the Esther story originally ended. Some scholars believe the story ended here. These scholars tend to take the conversion to Judaism as genuine, and point out that this makes the climax of the book the conversion of *the people of the country* (NRSV) or *other nationalities* (NIV)to Judaism.

Many commentators believe the original story included some or all of chapter 9. The climax of the book, they say, is not the conversion of the people to Judaism, but the slaughter of the enemies by the Jews. This is the ultimate turnabout in the book. These scholars, then, tend to see the conversion of the people of the country as a pretense. Just as Esther earlier had hidden her Jewishness, and lived as a non-Jew, so now the people of the country hid their non-Jewishness, and pretended to be Jews.

If the original story ended here, its purposes would have been to amuse and delight its Jewish readers, to instill in them a sense of pride and dignity, and to assure them of God's faithfulness in acting on behalf of the chosen people. With each addition to the text, we can discern additional purposes that the interpolaters probably had in mind. These are discussed in the commentary on 9:19; 9:20-32; 9:26; and 10:1-3. It should be noted, however, that some see the book of Esther as a unity, and deny that any portion of it was added later.

The Slaughter of the Enemies (9:1-15)

The edict of Mordecai empowered the Jews to defend themselves and to destroy any who attacked them; it did not give them permission to make the first strike. Nowhere in verses 2-4 is it said that the Jews were attacked, yet here *the Jews struck down all their enemies . . . and did what they pleased to those that hated them.* Perhaps we are to understand that the enemies struck the first blow, but we are never told that.

Three times we are told that the Jews laid no hand *on the plunder* (verses 10, 15, and 16). Perhaps the author wished to emphasize that the Jews were engaged in the slaughter only to protect their honor, and not for any personal gain.

Slaying *the ten sons of Haman* would have been seen by the Jews as a step toward blotting out the remembrance of Amalek from under heaven, a task they felt divinely called to do (see Exodus 17:14 and Deuteronomy 25:19).

According to verses 12-13, the king seemed horrified at the loss of so many men, yet, strangely, he asked Esther what else he could do to please her.

If Esther's request is historical, it is hard to see it as anything other than vindictive, though some might think of it as being a lesson to the enemies, or as a deterrent to future action. Her request that *the ten sons of Haman be hanged* is also vindictive. It is, in fact, pointless unless it is intended as a public example, for Haman's sons were already dead (verse 10). If, on the other hand, Esther's request is seen as serving a literary purpose, then it becomes understandable. It is, in fact, necessary to the story, for the author must explain to his readers why some Jews celebrated on the fourteenth day of Adar, and others on the fifteenth (verses 17-19).

The Celebration of Purim (9:16-32)

Seventy-five thousand (verse 16) is a large number to kill by sword and spear in one day.

Most scholars believe the book of Esther originally ended with verse 19 of chapter 9. Those who believe it ended after 8:17 see 9:1-19 as the first block of material to be added. The purposes of this addition were (1) to resolve the stalemate with which the story ended in 8:17, and (2) to give victory and justice to the Jewish people.

But there were other purposes as well. Apparently the Feast of Purim was an established tradition by the time the book of Esther was written. No one knew how or when the festival came into being, since it was not authorized by the books of Moses. The date of the feast varied from city to town, and no one knew why that was, either. These verses were added to the story, then, to explain all these things to the reader.

If 9:1-19 represents the first addition to the story of Esther, then 9:20-32 represents the second addition. If, however, the story originally ended at 9:19, as most scholars believe, verses 20-32 represent the first addition. Some scholars would divide 9:20-32 into two additions, verses 20-28 being the first, and verses 29-32 the second. Other commentators offer still more elaborate schemes.

Verses 1-19 explained the origin of the festival and why it was celebrated a day earlier in the rural areas than in the urban. But later it was no longer true that the festival was celebrated on the fourteenth of Adar in the towns, and on the fifteenth in the city. It was celebrated on both days in both places. Another addition to the story was needed, then, to explain how this happened.

There were other unanswered questions. Why was this festival called *Purim*? And why did it become an annual event? These questions are answered in verses 20-32.

In verses 20-22 are the answers to two of the questions. The festival is held each year, and it is held for two days each year because Mordecai mandated that it be. This, at least, was the first step in the process.

According to verse 23, the Jews agreed to do *as Mordecai had written*. They made the observance mandatory for themselves, their descendants, and all proselytes as well. That was the second step in institutionalizing this feast (that is, making it an annual festival)—not only did Mordecai mandate it; the people agreed to it. There will be yet a third step in verses 29-32.

Verses 24-25 give a brief summary of the story. Such a summary seems unnecessary, but its purpose is to lead into the explanation of the name of the feast.

This is the first time the word *crush* (NRSV) or *ruin* (NIV) has been used in connection with the pogrom. The author may be making a play on words, since the name *Haman* and the word *crush* are similar in Hebrew. The usual triple formula, "to destroy, to slay, and to annihilate," is missing.

It comes as a surprise to learn that *the king . . .* gave orders in writing that Haman should be executed. Nothing in chapter 7 would indicate that, and we certainly would not expect Ahasuerus to stop in the heat of his anger to write down his words of 7:10.

Verse 26 tells us why these days of celebration are called *Purim*. *Purim* is the plural of the word *pur*, the Persian word for *lot*. The casting of the lot, however, played a very minor role in the story. It was cast in 3:7, and this fact is mentioned again only in 9:24. Nowhere else were lots cast. It seems odd that a festival would be named after such an insignificant part of the story. Yet, if a festival named *Purim* existed in this author's day, it may well have seemed natural to him that this was the explanation for the name.

Some commentators find another problem with the name *Purim*, namely, that the plural *Purim* is used. The question arises because only one *pur* was cast. This need not confuse the reader, however, for although only one *pur* was cast, it was cast several times. It was cast for each month until the twelfth month was chosen, and cast for each day until the thirteenth day was selected.

However, it is probably a mistake to think the festival received its name from the casting of lots. Most Old Testament scholars believe *purim* had a non-Jewish origin. We know, for example, that the Babylonian New Year festivities included ceremonies designed to discover what lot or destiny the gods had for a person during the coming year. It is significant that the Jewish feast of Purim comes during Adar, the last month of the year. Perhaps behind the story of Esther stands a planned attack on the Jews that was averted during or just preceding the New Year festivities one of the years they were in exile. If so, it would be understandable that the name *Purim* would be given to a celebration of that event, for that would certainly portend a favorable lot for the Jews during the coming year. Furthermore, it would be understandable why such a festival would be celebrated annually just before the New Year.

In verses 29-32 we have the final stage in the institutionalizing of the feast of Purim. A *second letter* was sent out, this time by both Esther and Mordecai, ordering that *these days of Purim should* be observed.

The word *second* (verse 29) is not found in many of the ancient versions, and probably represents an addition to the text. The letter that Esther and Mordecai now sent was itself the *second letter*. It confirmed the first letter.

The words and Mordecai the Jew are probably secondary as well, for the verb is singular and in the feminine form.

In verse 31 is the first mention of the fasts and lamentations the people had *laid down for themselves* (NRSV) or *had decreed for them*. (NIV) The Talmud says the Jews should fast on the thirteenth of Adar and feast on the fourteenth and fifteenth.

The Greatness of Mordecai (10:1-3)

This appendix to the story of Esther highlights the honors bestowed on Mordecai. It also says to the Jews in exile that there is hope. For Mordecai was able to be popular with . . . his fellow Jews (10:3), retaining his Jewishness, while at the same time being elevated to second in command in the kingdom (10:2). The door to success is not barred shut by faithfulness to one's heritage.

§ § § § § § §

The Message of Esther 8–10

§ The edict of Mordecai in 8:11-12 is almost the exact counterpart of Haman's edict in 3:13. The Law of Talion (called *lex talionis*) said one should take a life for a life, an eye for an eye, a tooth for a tooth, or a hand for a hand (see Exodus 21:23-25; Leviticus 24:19-20; Deuteronomy 19:21). That is what Mordecai is doing here—he is matching Haman's edict point for point. The Law of Talion first arose, as far as we know, with Hammurabi. Its purpose was to make sure that revenge did not go beyond the bounds of justice.

According to the biblical text, Esther was not satisfied with the Law of Talion. Her request of Ahasuerus was that the Jews be allowed to go beyond the one-day limit imposed upon them by Mordecai's edict (9:13). When her request was granted, the Jews slew 300 more people in Susa the next day.

Jesus was not satisfied with the Law of Talion, either. But how different his dissatisfaction was! *You have heard that it was said, "an eye for an eye and a tooth for a tooth." But I say to you . . . "if any one strikes you on the right cheek, turn to him the other also"* (Matthew 5:38-39).

§ The author of 10:1-3 undoubtedly believed the high point of the book was Mordecai's elevation to second in command in the kingdom. Followers of Jesus are more apt to think the story reaches its climax when Mordecai, unlike his predecessor, unlike the king under whom he served, and unlike most high-ranking officials from that day to this, used his power not to serve himself, but to seek *the welfare of all* his people. That is a fine note on which to end the book.

§ § § § § § §

Glossary of Terms

Adar: The twelfth (last) month in the Hebrew calendar.
Beyond the River: The name given to the fifth Persian satrapy. The land west of the Euphrates River, including Palestine.
Booths, Feast of: One of three major annual festivals of the Israelites. Originally celebrated the closing of the agricultural year; adapted to commemorate the escape from Egypt.
Chaldeans: The people of the southernmost portion of the valley of the Tigris and Euphrates Rivers from about the eleventh century B.C. Also the restored Babylonian Empire in the seventh and sixth centuries B.C.
Chislev: The ninth month of the Hebrew calendar.
Daric: A Persian coin, the first coin mentioned in the Bible.
Edom: A country south of Moab, south and east of Judah, the home of the Edomites.
Elam: A country in the mountainous region east of the Tigris Valley, the home of the Elamites. Cyrus was king of Elam when he conquered Babylon and formed the Persian Empire.
Elephantine: An island in the Nile river near Aswan, the home of a Jewish colony during the Babylonian Exile. Important papyri have been discovered there.
Ephod: A small object consulted by priests to determine the divine will.
Esdras, First: A book in the Protestant Apocrypha, not found in the Roman Catholic Bible. It retells the story of Ezra, and in some places is better preserved than Ezra.
Grand Vizier: A prime minister, second in command.
Herodotus: Fifth-century B.C. Greek historian.

Hezekiah: King of Judah the last part of the eighth century and the first part of the seventh century B.C.

Jamnia, Council of: A meeting of Jewish leaders in A.D. 90 during which several books were admitted to the canon.

Levite: An order in the Israelite cult considered above the laity, but below the priests.

Maccabees, First and Second: Books in the Protestant Apocrypha and in the Roman Catholic canon.

Marduk: The supreme god of Babylon.

Media: A country extending from the Zagros Mountains to the Caspian Sea, the home of the Medes. Conquered by Cyrus, and made a part of the Persian Empire.

Mesopotamia: Literally "Between Rivers," a country located between the Tigris and the Euphrates Rivers.

Nebuchadnezzar: Also Nebuchadrezzar, King of Babylon when Judah was defeated and her people taken into exile in 587.

Nisan: The first month of the Hebrew calendar.

Origen: Third-century Christian scholar and teacher.

Purim: The Persian word, *pur*, with the Hebrew plural ending, *im*. Refers to the two-day festival in celebration of the victory of Esther and Mordecai over Haman.

Samaritans: Descendants of the Israelites who were not deported at the fall of Samaria in 722 B.C., and the non-Israelite pagans who were brought in from other portions of the Assyrian Empire.

Satrap: A Persian official, ruler of a satrapy, a governor.

Sidon: City in Phoenicia, home of the Sidonians, who were known as skilled carpenters and masons.

Sivan: The third month of the Hebrew calendar.

Tishri: The seventh month of the Hebrew calendar.

Tyropoeon Valley: Valley which divides Ophel from the Upper City of Jerusalem.

Urim and Thummim: Small objects used in discovering the divine will by casting lots.

Vulgate: Latin translation of the Bible by Jerome in the fourth century.

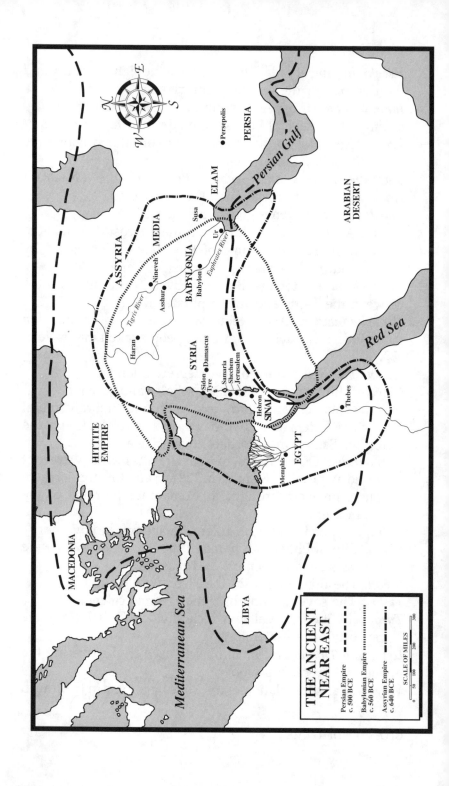

THE ANCIENT
NEAR EAST

Persian Empire
c. 500 BCE

Babylonian Empire
c. 560 BCE

Assyrian Empire
c. 640 BCE

SCALE OF MILES

0 50 100   200   300